Illustrated
MERCEDES-BENZ
BUYER'S GUIDE T.M.

Illustrated

MERCEDES-BENZ
BUYER'S GUIDE™

Motorbooks International
Publishers & Wholesalers Inc
Osceola, Wisconsin 54020, USA ®

First published in 1986 by Motorbooks
International Publishers & Wholesalers Inc, PO
Box 2, 729 Prospect Avenue, Osceola, WI 54020
USA

Printed and bound in the United States of
America

The information in this book is true and
complete to the best of our knowledge. All
recommendations are made without any
guarantee on the part of the author or
publisher, who also disclaim any liability
incurred in connection with the use of this data
or specific details

Library of Congress Cataloging in Publication Data
Gohlike, Lee
   Illustrated Mercedes-Benz buyer's guide.
   1. Mercedes automobile. I. Title.
TL215.M4G63 1983 629.2'222   82-14431
ISBN 0-87938-162-0 (soft)

Cover photo: 1971 280SE 3.5 convertible,
by Tim Parker

To Linda, Frank and Adele

Many people gave assistance during this proj-
ect with its special circumstances, for which
I am very grateful. I would like to give
appropriate thanks to the following: Ann
Bergman, DBAG's archives, Alex Dearborn,
Barbara Harold, Bill Kosfeld, Bill Krause,
Tim Parker.

Contents

Why Mercedes-Benz?

Carl Benz is credited with building the world's first automobile in 1885. Gottlieb Daimler produced his first car one year later, in 1886. In 1926, Daimler Motoren Gesellschaft, which had named its most successful model after Mercedes Jellinek, the daughter of an important customer, merged with Firma Benz & Cie to form Daimler-Benz using the trade name Mercedes-Benz.

Carl Benz, born in 1844, lived to see the merger, but Gottlieb Daimler died in 1900 at the age of sixty-six. At the time of the merger, the strongest engineering influence was Ferdinand Porsche. Originally hired in 1923 by the Daimler company, Porsche started work on the Mercedes Type 400, the beginning of one of the most important series of sports cars ever produced.

The Type 400, introduced in 1924, was an entirely new four-liter supercharged car. It was immediately followed by the first Mercedes-Benz automobile, the model 630, and a shortened model K in 1926. These set the stage for the S, SS, SSK and SSKL whose greatness lay in Porsche engineering that combined sports car elegance with proven Grand Prix racing technology. (During this special time, anyone with the desire and a pocketbook could purchase a Grand Prix automobile directly off the showroom floor.)

The concept of breeding racing technology with sports car construction changed in 1933 with Hitler's program for Grand Prix racing. Large monetary rewards justified research and development solely for racing and thus separated the racing department from sports car development. In 1934, the Daimler-Benz racing division introduced the sophisticated 354 hp eight-cylinder W-25, while sports car enthusiasts had to be happy with the moderately powered but pleasant looking 120 hp supercharged type 380. This pattern continued until World War II brought both forms of development to a halt.

The Mercedes-Benz plant suffered major destruction during the war. Afterward, Daimler-Benz picked up the pieces and started over. Using prewar parts, machines and engineering, it produced a small number of 170Vs to generate cash flow and progressed rapidly. By 1952, Mercedes introduced the modern successor to the SSK and SSKL: the 300SL and 300SLR.

Development through the 1950s and 1960s to the present has been a consistent success story. Mercedes-Benz prospered using tried-and-tested engineering and successful models—never changing for change itself, but only when something truly better was developed. This is illustrated not only in mechanical development but also in styling. Mercedes-Benz' practice has been to introduce styling changes in the sports car models, and only later, after careful study, apply them to the standard sedan line. This practice has maintained the obvious continuity in Mercedes-Benz styling.

The purpose of this book is to provide an identification and buying-as-an-investment guide. Much of the text emphasizes individual component differences for ready identification and straightforward, comparative investment information. There is not much room here for dreaming, and therefore little time is spent describing cars which you won't see, let alone purchase. No known prototypes are described nor are specific military, competition or commercial vehicles.

Prewar cars, because of their age, rarity and expense, present special problems—if not in purchase, then in restoration. Several series are singled out, however, because they are highly desirable and glamorous, and because they gather crowds wherever they go. These cars seldom change hands, and when they do, it is among a select few who usually have wealth and knowledge on their side.

The postwar series of Mercedes-Benz cars are complex and sections on these will take a certain amount of careful reading. Mercedes-Benz has used an almost exclusive model-numbering system related to the engine capacity and/or body style. This means a typical model number can have been used for nearly thirty years and have covered five body styles, perhaps two of those body styles simultaneously. Sound confusing?

The mass-produced sedans and all the diesels are grouped in one chapter because they are not collector/investor cars and are unlikely to become so. From a practical point of view, these cars must be seen mainly as "interesting" transportation. The diesel coupes are an exception, and will appreciate.

Identification

In order to make the identification of modern Mercedes-Benz automobiles easier I have had to devise a system for categorizing the cars by body style. That may sound quite simple when dealing with coupes, convertibles, SLs and even gullwing coupes but it is very difficult when it comes to sedans. For that reason I have concentrated on sorting out the rather complex sedans. Please understand that some of the descriptive terms are my own.

The following do not directly tie-in with chapter titles and contents. Since instant, visual identification by body style is often difficult, further analysis by engine and chassis must be done to determine just what you are looking at. That is why I have further categorized the cars by engine/chassis, and it also explains why two or more body styles will be mentioned in one chapter.

Body style

The production Mercedes-Benz models are sorted into eighteen different body styles: ten prewar and eight postwar.

A. Prewar six-cylinder supercharged
  1. High profile: 400, 630 and K
    a. Tall radiators, hood and body
    b. Very vee'd radiators with two star logos
    c. Very small knock-off hubs
    d. External exhaust pipe on K only
  2. S series: S, SS, SSK and SSKL
    a. Three external exhaust pipes
    b. Small knock-off hubs
    c. Low profile, with the S and SSK very low and the SS three inches taller
    d. Two star logos on the S radiator; one star logo on the SS, SSK, and SSKL

B. Prewar unblown
  1. Square body: 300, early 320 and 350
    a. Very square line with totally vertical windshield
    b. Flat, vertical radiators
  2. Stuttgart: 200 and 260
    a. Body line slightly more rounded than square
    b. Flat, vertical radiators
  3. Nurburg: 460 and 500
    a. Large cars
    b. Slightly vee'd radiators, slightly tapered backs
    c. Relatively small knock-off hubs
  4. Mannheim: 350, 370, 370K, 370S and 380S
    a. Generally beautiful, rounded body lines
    b. Flat, vertical radiators
  5. Mid-30: 170, 200, 230, 290 and 320
    a. Seventeen-inch disc wheels on most
    b. Snap-on hubcaps
    c. Tapered radiators
    d. Tapered windshields
  6. Diesel
    a. Usually Pullman or landaulette
    b. Diesel script on radiator

7. Rear engine: 130, 150 and 170H
   a. Very small, Volkswagen-type bodies

C. Prewar eight-cylinder supercharged
   1. Kompressor series: 380, 500K, 540K, 570K and 770K
      a. External exhaust pipes on all but 380
      b. Large knock-off hubs with seventeen-inch wire wheels
      c. Vee'd and tapered-back radiator with single star logo

D. Early postwar
   1. Suicide doors: 170V (prewar and postwar), 170Va, 170Vb, 170S, 170Sb, 170SV and 220
      a. Front door opens from the front of the car
   2. Bathtub: 180, 180a, 180b, 180c, 190, 190b, 220a, 219, 220S, 220SE, 300, 300b, 300c, 300d, 300S and 300SC
      a. Very rounded bodies with incorporated fenders
      b. Single built-in headlights

E. Postwar sports
   1. Gullwing: 300SL
      a. Gullwing doors
   2. SL: 190SL, 300SL, 230SL, 250SL, 280SL, 350SL, 450SL, 380SL and 500SL
      a. Internal radiator
      b. Oval front grille with large star logo
   3. Fin style: 190, 200, 220b, 220S, 220SEb, 230, 230S, 300SE and 300SEL
      a. Very pronounced rear fender tails
   4. Squareline: 220, 230, 250, 250C, 250CE, 280 and 280E
      a. Square front fender and headlight doors
      b. Chamfered rear fenders with no fin
   5. Highline: 220SE coupe and convertible; 250SE coupe and convertible; 280SE coupe and convertible; 280SE 3.5 coupe and convertible; 300SE 3.0, 3.5, 4.5, sedan, coupe and convertible; and 600, 300SEL and 6.3
      a. Pear-shaped headlight doors and front fenders
      b. Round rear fenders with slight fin

6. Postwar S-class: 280S; 280SE; 450SE; 450SEL; 450SLC and 6.9; 380SE, SEL, SLC, SEC; and 500SE, SEL, SLC, SEC
   a. Aerodynamic body line
   b. Square headlight doors

Body type

1. Cabriolet
A convertible with a year-round, all-weather convertible top. The tops are usually padded with horsehair or similar padding. Because of their weight, landau irons are used to help support the tops while going up and down.

Cabriolet A: Cabriolet with two doors and room for two passengers; often has room for one more passenger seated sideways behind the front seats

Cabriolet B: Cabriolet with two doors and room for four or five passengers; fitted with a rear quarter window for the rear seat

Cabriolet C: Cabriolet with two doors and room for four or five passengers with no rear quarter window

Cabriolet D: Cabriolet with four doors and room for four or five passengers

2. Open touring
Normally a two-door with a very lightweight top, side curtains and room for four or five passengers.

3. Roadster
Two-door, two-passenger convertible with a more or less disappearing top. Special roadsters featured special fenders, windshields and other stylistic details.

4. Coupe
A two-door hardtop.

Coupe A: Two-door coupe with room for two or three passengers

Coupe B: Two-door coupe with room for four or five passengers; also called a saloon

5. Sedan
A four-door hardtop with room for four or five passengers and a separate trunk in the rear.

6. Sportwagen

Four- or five-passenger with no doors, or two small doors in the rear; for sports car racing formulas requiring four passengers.

Chassis and engine numbers

Understanding the engine and chassis codes will also be helpful in identifying post-1945 Mercedes-Benz models.

Chassis numbers always used 0 or 1 as the fourth digit; engine numbers always used 9.

Both chassis and engine numbers used eleven digits from 1946 to 1950. These consisted of the basic type, model style and then serial number.

For 1951 and 1952 cars, the production year was added, making thirteen digits.

For 1953 through (including) 1959, thirteen digits were retained but code letters were added for clutch and transmission types, and the year of production digits were reversed.

Fourteen digits were used from 1960 on. The year of production digits were eliminated and the code letters were changed to numbers. Regardless of the year of manufacture, each model was numbered consecutively, making a six-digit serial number.

Here's an example (actually a 1980 300CD).
Chassis number: 12315012005611
123 — chassis type
150 — model type
1 — left-hand drive
2 — automatic transmission
005611 — serial number
Engine number: 61791212098083
617 — engine type
912 — model type
1 — left-hand drive
2 — automatic transmission
098083 — serial number

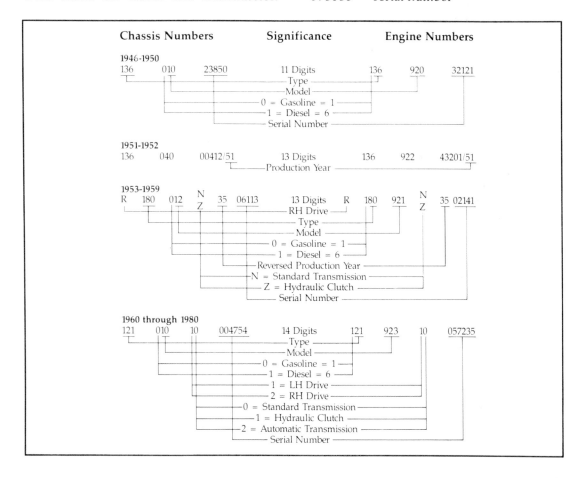

A seventeen-digit system was started in 1981 and Vehicle Identification Numbers (VIN) were found on the left-side windshield pillar and on the left front door post. The VIN can determine whether a car is to US specification or a foreign model, its original restraint system, build plant, model year, even its place in the production run.

VIN and vehicle serial numbers should conform to those shown here, for the years 1981 through 1985. The T in the model column means turbo. The numbers shown are samples only.

Both charts are courtesy *The Star* and MBNA, with thanks.

Model	1981 Model Year	1982 Model Year	1983 Model Year	1984 Model Year	1985 Model Year
190E 2.3				WDBDA24A1EB123456	WDBDA24C1FF123456
190D 2.2				WDBDB22A1EB123456	WDBDB22C1FF123456
240D	WDBAB23A1BB123456	WDBAB23A1CB123456	WDBAB23A1DB123456		
280E	WDBAA33A1BB123456				
280CE	WDBAA53A1BB123456				
300D	WDBAB30A1BB123456				
300D (T)		WDBAB33A1CB123456	WDBAB33A1DB123456	WDBAB33A1EB123456	WDBAB33C1FA123456
300TD (T)	WDBAB93A1BN123456	WDBAB93A1CN123456	WDBAB93A1DN123456	WDBAB93A1EN123456	WDBAB93C1FF123456
300CD	WDBAB50A1BB123456				
300CD (T)		WDBAB53A1CB123456	WDBAB53A1DB123456	WDBAB53A1EB123456	WDBAB53A1FA123456
300SD (T)	WDBCB20A1BB123456	WDBCB20A1CB123456	WDBCB20A1DB123456	WDBCB20A1EB123456	WDBCB20C1FA123456
380SEL	WDBCA33A1BB123456	WDBCA33A1CB123456	WDBCA33A1DB123456		
380SE				WDBCA32A1EB123456	WDBCA32C1FA123456
380SEC		WDBCA43A1CB123456	WDBCA43A1DB123456		
380SL	WDBBA45A1BB123456	WDBBA45A1CB123456	WDBBA45A1DB123456	WDBBA45A1EB123456	WDBBA45C1FA123456
380SLC	WDBBA25A1BB123456				
500SEL				WDBCA37A1EB123456	WDBCA37D1FA123456
500SEC				WDBCA44A1EB123456	WDBCA44D1FA123456

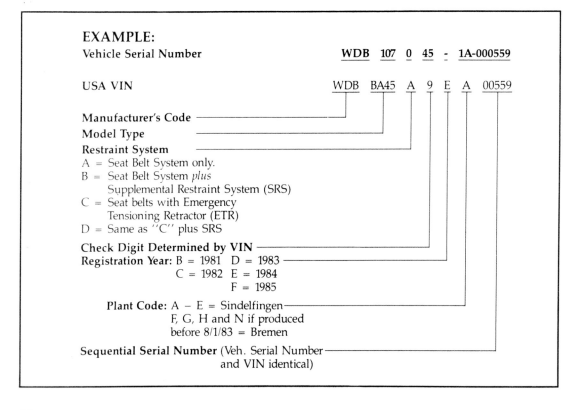

EXAMPLE:

Vehicle Serial Number   **WDB** **107** **0** **45** - **1A-000559**

USA VIN   WDB BA45 A 9 E A 00559

Manufacturer's Code ——————

Model Type ——————

Restraint System ——————
A = Seat Belt System only.
B = Seat Belt System *plus*
     Supplemental Restraint System (SRS)
C = Seat belts with Emergency
     Tensioning Retractor (ETR)
D = Same as ''C'' plus SRS

Check Digit Determined by VIN ——————
Registration Year: B = 1981   D = 1983 ——————
                C = 1982   E = 1984
                F = 1985

Plant Code: A − E = Sindelfingen ——————
      F, G, H and N if produced
      before 8/1/83 = Bremen

Sequential Serial Number (Veh. Serial Number ——————
           and VIN identical)

European Models / U.S. Models
1981-1982-1983-1984-1985-1986-1987 Model Years

Model	Model ID	Available in Europe	81	82	83	84	85	86	87	
190	201.022	Thru /84								
190/1	201.	From /84								
190E	201.024	Thru /82								
190E 2.3	201.024	From /85				X	X	X	X	
190E 2.6	201.	From 9/85							X	
190E 2.3-16	201.034	From 9/83						X	X	
190D	201.122	From /82								
190D 2.2	201.122					X	X	X		
190D 2.5	201.	From 4/85							X	
190D 2.5 (T)	201.								X	
200	123.220	Thru /85								
200	124.020	From /84								
200T	123.280	Thru /85								
200T	124.	From /84								
200D	123.120	Thru /85								
200D	124.120	From 1/85								
200TD	124.	From 1/85								
230	123.023	Thru /85								
230TE	123.283	Thru /85								
230TE	124.	From 1/85								
230E	123.223	Thru /85								
230E	124.023	From /84								
230CE	123.234	Thru /85								
240TD	123.183	Thru /85								
240D	123.123	Thru /85	X	X	X					
250	123.026	Thru /85								
250D	124.125	From 1/85								
250T	123.086	Thru 8/82								
250TD	124.	From /85								
260E	124.026	From 1/85						X		
260TE	124.	From 1/85								
280	123.030	Thru 8/81								
280E	123.033	Thru /85	X							
280CE	123.053	Thru /85	X							
280TE	123.093	Thru /85								
280S	126.021	Thru /85								
280SE	126.022	Thru /85								
280SEL	126.023	Thru /85								
280SLC	107.022	Thru 8/81								
280SL	107.042	Thru /85								
300E	124.030	From 1/85						X	X	
300TE	124.	From /85								

Model	Model ID	Available in Europe	Available as a U.S. model in model year:							
			81	82	83	84	85	86	87	
300SE	126.	From /85								
300SEL	126.	From /85								
300D	123.130	Thru /85	X							
300D	124.130	From /84								
300D (T)	123.133	Thru /85		X	X	X	X			
300D (T)	124.	From /86						X	X	
300TD	123.190	Thru 1/85								
300TD	124.	From 1/85								
300TD (T)	123.193	Thru /85	X	X	X	X	X			
300TD (T)	124.	From /86						X	X	
300CD	123.150	Thru /81	X							
300CD (T)	123.153	Thru /85		X	X	X	X			
300SD (T)	126.120		X	X	X	X	X			
300SDL (T)	126.							X	X	
300SL	107.	From 1/85								
380SE	126.032	Thru /85				X	X			
380SEL	126.033	Thru /85	X	X	X					
380SEC	126.043	Thru /85		X	X					
380SL	107.045	Thru /85	X	X	X	X	X			
380SLC	107.025	Thru 8/81	X							
420SE	126.	From /85								
420SEL	126.	From /85							X	
420SEC	126.	From /85								
420SL	107.	From /85								
500SE	126.036	Thru /85								
500SEL	126.037	Thru /85				X	X			
500SEC	126.044	Thru /85				X	X			
500SL	107.046	Thru /85								
500SLC	107.026	Thru 8/81								
560SEL	126.	From /85						X	X	
560SEC	126.	From /85								
560SL	107.	From /85						X	X	
600	100.012	Thru 8/81						X	X	

How to buy a collector Mercedes-Benz

Buying a Mercedes-Benz is not very different from buying any other car, although there are a few special considerations. As you look for a particular car, you may find that the search is almost as rewarding as the find. Break your search down into three stages: advance work, examining the car and making the deal.

Advance work

a. Decide what you want: look, listen, then drive. Since there are so many Mercedes-Benz models, it can be difficult deciding which one is right for you. This is where publications and clubs can be of assistance. Also talk to new- and used-car dealers who carry the model you like. Ask yourself how you will use the car; it's a shame to drive a valuable car to work in rotten weather. Do you want a sports car or a sedan? Can you afford to maintain an elaborate model? Are you interested in performance, comfort, styling or practicality?

b. Decide how much you want to spend, arrange financing and work out a budget for acquisition and restoration (if needed). If you are borrowing money, talk to your banker and other lending sources well in advance of the time you will need the money. Some banks specialize in collector car loans. Leasing may be an alternative.

If you are buying a car from out of town, there are ways to escrow your money in the seller's bank so you can approve its release after you have examined the car or had it appraised.

c. Find an expert to give you some advice; again, clubs may be helpful. If your car will need restoration, talk to experienced restorers to estimate possible costs. Always keep in mind that special problems will materialize during a thorough restoration. Also let dealers know you are looking for a car, so they can keep an eye open.

d. Start looking for available cars in newspapers, magazines and club newsletters. Local newspapers are often overlooked as good sources because everyone assumes you must look in more exotic places for this type of car. There are plenty of less expensive Mercedes-Benzes listed in small papers all over the country.

Examining the car

a. Have an expert help you examine the car. You may have to pay the mechanic or restorer a small fee, but it is well worth it. An impartial opinion costs you practically nothing compared to what you may lose on a basket case. If you check the car out yourself, use the following guidelines.

b. Look closely, always take notes and be objective. Don't let your imagination get the better of you. Write down everything that may need repair or that puzzles you and discuss these items with the owner. Make note of the chassis and engine numbers so that you can check them against reference lists.

Look for rust or body damage. Since mechanical repairs are less costly than body repairs, it is always best to look for a car with a solid body.

Many Mercedes-Benz models are susceptible to rust, so always check the undercarriage. In earlier models, make sure the cross-members of the frame are solid and strong. In models with unibody construction, first appearing in 1954, rust can nearly destroy the structural rigidity of the entire car. Check the front cross-member and all body seams. Check floor pans, and use a flashlight to inspect hidden areas. Be especially skeptical of fresh undercoating, welds or other signs of repair.

While under the car, check the exhaust system for rust or improper repairs. Many Mercedes exhaust systems are welded together, and parts are costly, so it is not unusual to find some unique repairs.

Many Mercedes-Benzes featured aluminum body panels, usually doors, rocker panels and hood and trunk lids. These will not rust, but they dent far more easily than steel panels and should be thoroughly examined. Body damage repaired with body filler can be detected with a small magnet; check the aluminum panels for body filler, too!

Chrome replacement pieces can be hard to find, and expensive, for any model you are thinking of. Examine all the chrome trim and especially the grille. Throughout the book these types of trim pieces are described as either scarce or expensive, or both.

Look for oil leaks at the front and rear seals of the engine. These leaks may indicate the seals need replacing, from blow-by caused by bad piston rings. Check the brake cylinders, calipers and lines for fluid leaks as well.

This is a good time to check the wheel bearings. Grasp each tire firmly at the top and bottom and try to rock it on the axle—it shouldn't rock. If the car has a hydraulic compensator above the differential, it should not allow the car's tail to sag. If the car has flexible couplings on the driveshaft and steering column, look for torn fiber or any evidence of failure.

Ask for any maintenance records and talk to whoever did the work. Many Mercedes-Benz owners keep excellent records of maintenance and repairs. Examining them also allows you to subtly check the accuracy of the odometer reading.

If the battery is in the right cowl above the passenger footwell, lift the battery and look for corrosion. Check the carpet and floor mat on the passenger side for evidence of coolant or battery acid. Look for sloppy wiring and signs of amateur repairs such as rounded bolt heads, duct tape and baling wire.

c. Drive the car—that is, if it runs. Aside from checking the car's operation, you may find that your favorite Mercedes-Benz is not for you. Too slow, too fast, too big, too small, or maybe not fun to drive.

Start the car when the engine is cold and pay attention to the oil pressure gauge. Postwar Mercedes cars usually hit maximum oil pressure right away and do not drop off until the car is idling hot. Once you have a hot idle, rev the engine just above idle; the oil pressure gauge should immediately hit maximum. If this does not happen, the car could have bad engine bearings or a weak or faulty oil pump.

Watch the temperature gauge, too. The car should run quite cool until driven hard. Some older six-cylinder cars can get hot quickly if the water pump or radiator are in poor condition. Once the car is warm but not running, feel the radiator hoses; if they are spongy or cracked, you will have to replace them. No big deal, but a good point to bring up during negotiations. Look for signs of coolant leaks on hose joints and the radiator. If the fan is mounted on the water pump shaft, try to wiggle it to check for wear.

Try the radio, tape deck, sunroof, air conditioning, power windows, power seats, heater and so on. Do all the instruments work? Interior lights, switches and locks? Does the trunk contain the spare wheel, tool kit, jack and lug wrench? Many postwar cars have wells on both sides of the trunk floor. Hidden beneath the trunk mat is a wooden cover; lift these out and look for rust.

Check the fluid in the brake hydraulic clutch reservoirs. If the car was maintained regularly, the fluid was changed frequently and therefore should be clear. If the car has a vacuum power brake booster, does it work?

Do the windshield wipers and washer

work properly? Do all the lights work?

    d. Test the engine. Check the condition of the rings and valves with a compression test and a leakdown test. This can be a bit difficult and I recommend you consult a qualified Mercedes-Benz mechanic.

Making the deal

    a. Think about the deal. Why is the owner selling, what does the car need, will the owner negotiate? Figure the cost of repairs or restoration versus the value of the car. Is the owner trying to pressure you, what does

PROBLEM	SOLUTION	MODELS AFFECTED
Unibody rust	Cut out affected part; replace with new or fabricated parts	Most models after 1954 except 300 series
Wood frame rot	Remove sheet metal; buy or make new wood frame parts from ash; assemble and replace	Prewar convertibles plus 170 and 200 cabriolet As
Ineffective chassis lubrication by central lube pump	Disconnect terminal ends; run kerosene through line; pump dry and top with 90 wt gear lube	Most prewar models plus 170, 220 and 300 model of the 1950s
Transmission pops out of gear, mostly in 4th	Install new syncromesh rings in affected gears	All postwar models with standard transmissions
Brake fluid loss and white exhaust smoke	Replace vacuum brake booster, diaphragm with rebuilt kit	Most postwar models from 1955 on
Locked brakes	Replace rubber brake lines	All pre-1960 models
Loud rear axle	Adjust heel or toe contact in differential	All
Car bounces on bumps	Replace shock absorbers	All
Front wheels shimmy at certain speeds	Replace worn front axle parts; check tire balance	All
Low oil pressure	Check and replace main or rod bearings; grind crank	All
Low compression	Check piston rings or valves with cylinder leakdown test	All
Engine stops but has fuel and spark	Replace timing chain (it is slipping)	All overhead cam engines
Standard transmission is hard to shift	Adjust shift linkage	All with linkage-type transmissions
Fuel line blockage	Change fuel filter, remove fuel tank and have cleaned	Cars stored over two years
Uneven tire wear	Check wheel alignment, tire balance and shocks	All

he or she want out of the deal, will the owner take a note at low interest, deferred payments or trades?

b. Negotiate. Discuss the needs of the car diplomatically and explain how you figure repair and restoration costs and refer to some current price guide if possible. Know in your mind what you are willing to pay. Walk away if you have to, and tell the owner to call in a week or so if the car is still available. Be polite but firm, and explain your reasoning.

c. Make sure the owner has legal right to the car and that there are not liens on it.

Investment rating

Mercedes-Benz engineering makes sure that there are no Mercedes-Benz "dogs." Every car works. Some work better than others, some are faster or more economical than others—but they all work. At least they did when they were new. As anything other than simple transportation, some Mercedes are not good investments. On the other hand, some are magnificent investments.

This buyer's guide uses a five-star rating system to help you pick particular models as collector car investments. The rating system is justified as follows:

★★★★★ High performance, elegant styling and/or rarity.
★★★★ Moderate performance and elegant styling.
★★★ Moderate performance and good styling.
★★ Moderate performance and poor, or utility, styling.
★ Poor performance and poor styling.

The open stars indicate a further status of your investment. The more open stars the better—especially on the most expensive models.

This rating system has a bias for rarity (more stars); therefore, the low-production coupes and convertibles rate better than mass-production sedans.

Finally, it is fair to say not everyone is going to agree with these general ratings which have been created to help you spot sound investment potential. A four-door-model 200 diesel may be a very nice car, but even though it is a Mercedes, it is not a collector car.

Chapter 1

Prewar six-cylinder supercharged

This series of cars, designed by Ferdinand Porsche, represents the greatest of the grand sports cars of the time produced by Mercedes-Benz. These cars were designed as sports/racing cars, and their success on the track created a market among the sporting rich of the world.

K, 1926-29

The six-cylinder model K (Kurz) was Mercedes-Benz's first commercially successful supercharged sports car. Although the K appeared to be quite large, it was actually a shortened version of the model 630. The model K derived its name from the German word *Kurz,* meaning shorter. (The K has no relationship to the K used in the 380, 500, 540, 580 and 770K, which designated "kompressor." The K is included here with the S series cars because it was such an immediate precursor to the S.)

Aside from some minor differences in engine bore and carburetion, the model K used nearly the same engine and supercharger as the immortal SSK. Thus, the model K was quite a performer.

The majority of the model Ks were fitted with the sporty, four-passenger open tourer

TYPE: K	
ENGINE	
Type	6-cyl 6.25-ltr
Bore x stroke	94 x 150 mm
Displacement	6240 cc
Compression ratio	1:5.0
Horsepower	160 hp@3100 rpm
Torque	44 mkg@1400 rpm
CHASSIS & DRIVETRAIN	
Transmission	4-speed manual
Rear axle ratio	3.28
GENERAL	
Wheelbase	3400 mm
Track, front and rear	1430 mm
Weight	2000 kg
Maximum speed	145 km/h
Fuel consumption	25 ltr/100 km
Gas tank capacity	140 ltr

☆☆☆☆☆	**SSKL**
☆☆☆★★	**SS factory roadster and SSK factory race car**
☆☆★★★	**SS factory cabriolet A and SSK factory sports body**
☆★★★★	**S factory sports/racer**
★★★★★	**S factory open tourer, S custom body, SSK custom body, SS factory sportwagen, SS factory open tourer and SS custom body**
★★★★	**K**

bodies. The K motor produced 160 hp, compared with the 180 hp engine of the early model S. Weights were also comparable, with the 4,500 pound model K open tourer

This early factory-bodied model K carries wooden wheels; wires were also available. Notice the higher profile; it is this more than anything else which distinguishes the K from its successor, the S. Still a good buy for the money, the K is a generally undervalued car. (Mercedes-Benz)

TYPE: S	
ENGINE	
Type	6-cyl 6.8-ltr
Bore x stroke	98x150 mm
Displacement	6800 cc
Valve operation	single overhead cam, gear driven
Compression ratio	1:6.2
Horsepower	225 hp@3200 rpm
Torque	46.2 mkg@1900 rpm
CHASSIS & DRIVETRAIN	
Clutch	multidisc dry
Transmission	4-speed manual
Rear suspension	straight axle with leaf springs
Rear axle ratio	2.50, 2.76 or 3.09
Front suspension	solid axle with leaf springs
GENERAL	
Wheelbase	3400 mm
Track, front and rear	1420 mm
Tire size, front and rear	6.50x20
Weight	1950 kg
Maximum speed	190 km/h
Fuel consumption	27 ltr/100 km
Gas tank capacity	130 ltr

The S sportwagen in full racing trim. This was the first body type used by Mercedes on the S model and although it was designed specifically for the sports car racing formula, it remains today one of the most beautiful sports cars ever built. With elegant lines and sophisticated mechanics, it has everything! (Mercedes-Benz)

being just 200 pounds heavier than the S open tourer.

Although the K and S models were very similar, the higher profile of the K was a handicap in fast cornering. The K is a very desirable and rare car, with just 150 produced. In terms of value, the K is slightly behind its successor, the S.

S, 1926-30

The first S (Super) models were designed as factory racing cars. Records show that some early S models also used the small-bore K engine but were modified with twin carburetors.

The S model's 1-2-3 victory in the 1927 German Grand Prix at Nurburgring was a great debut for this incredible series of cars. Many knowledgeable Mercedes enthusiasts consider the S series to be the greatest expression of the grand sports car. The 155 S models produced are among the most-sought-after and valuable cars in existence.

Normally, factory-bodied Mercedes are more desirable than the special-bodied cars. There are, however, several very beautiful S models with special coachwork. This unmistakable Saouchik is definitely one of them. The S is considered by many to be better proportioned with its low hoodline than the SS. (Mercedes-Benz)

The factory-bodied S open tourer offered a little more comfort for the sportsman of the road. Several of these beautiful models exist today in original condition and I am sure these grand sports cars will be preserved for future generations.

Surprisingly, the S is a full three inches lower than its successor, the model SS. Although the S used the smaller-bore engine, its long, low lines make it just as desirable as the SS. In general, the S models were fitted with lighter and simpler bodies than the SS. The S is your choice if you are looking for more sportiness in a four-passenger vintage sports car.

The model S had many subtle differences from its successors, the SS and SSK. These differences are important when checking originality and correctness of any S-series car. They included oil pan, intake manifolds, valves, cam, transmission, axles, shocks and many minor details.

The S was offered with the following factory bodies as well as a multitude of custom bodies: racing sportwagen, early- and late-version open tourer, and cabriolet C.

SS, 1927-35

The SS (Super Sport) is considered a

This very special factory-bodied SS cabriolet A is a very late development model and therefore one of the most desirable. Lovingly stored by a Chicago collector for over 20 years it is now in Germany under restoration.

TYPE: SS	
ENGINE	
Type	6-cyl 7.1-ltr
Bore x stroke	100x150 mm
Displacement	7065 cc
Valve operation	single overhead cam, gear driven
Compression ratio	1:6.2
Horsepower	225 hp@3300 rpm
Torque	46.2 mkg @1900 rpm
CHASSIS & DRIVETRAIN	
Clutch	multidisc dry
Transmission	4-speed manual
Rear suspension	straight axle, leaf springs
Rear axle ratio	2.48 or 2.55
Front suspension	solid axle, leaf springs
GENERAL	
Wheelbase	3400 mm
Track, front and rear	1420 mm
Tire size, front and rear	6.50x20
Maximum speed	190 km/h
Fuel consumption	27 ltr/100 km
Gas tank capacity	130 ltr

This 1933 SS special roadster was built as a show piece to late-development SS production. This particular car was used as a show car by Mercedes-Benz until it was sold in 1936, probably the last S-series car sold by the factory. Notice the front fender; this is one of two types used on all SS factory-bodied, late-development cars. (Mercedes-Benz)

grand sports touring car, compared with the model S grand sports car and the model SSK grand sports racing car.

The radiator of the SS was three inches higher than that of the S and SSK models to accommodate larger, more comfortable bodies. These larger bodies meant some sacrifice in performance and cornering ability. Most SS models were fitted with road bodies and elegant interior trim. The most interesting bodies, along with the custom bodies, were the cabriolet As and roadsters.

Although the SS was available with heavier touring bodies, it was a very successful racing car in lighter, racing coachwork. The notorious "elephant" blower that was offered on the SSK was also available on the SS. This ominous blower had eighteen cooling fins, compared with fifteen on the standard model. When fitted with this blower and the higher-compression engine, the SS could produce approximately 250 hp.

The S series reached its highest stage of development with a series of later SS cars built from 1931 to 1934. A total of 107 SS models were produced overall. As with most series, late-development cars are more desirable than earlier models.

SSK, 1928-34

The SSK (Super Sport Kurz) was developed for grand prix racing using an S frame shortened approximately seventeen inches

and a larger-bore SS engine. Records show a total of thirty-three SSKs were commissioned for production. Records also show additional S and SS cars were converted to SSKs, so the exact number produced is hard to determine.

To further complicate things, several S and SS cars were shortened to SSK length by their owners for racing, and several more S and SS cars were also converted to SSKs in postwar years. There is no question that more SSKs exist today than the factory orig-

TYPE: SSK	
ENGINE	
Type	6-cyl 7.1-ltr
Bore x stroke	100x150 mm
Displacement	7065 cc
Valve operation	single overhead cam gear driven
Compression ratio	1:6
Horsepower	250 hp@3300 rpm
Torque	57.3 mkg@1900 rpm
CHASSIS & DRIVETRAIN	
Clutch	multidisc dry
Transmission	4-speed manual
Rear suspension	straight axle with leaf springs
Rear axle ratio	2.50 or 3.09
Front suspension	solid axle with leaf springs
GENERAL	
Wheelbase	2950 mm
Track, front and rear	1420 mm
Tire size, front and rear	6.50x20
Weight	1700 kg
Maximum speed	188 km/h
Fuel consumption	27 ltr/100 km
Gas tank capacity	130 ltr

This is the same car as was found in the south of France in 1978.

The SS special roadster in restored condition.

inally produced. The chances of an original SSK being offered on the market are very slim. However, it is possible that converted cars will become available from time to time.

The life! This factory-bodied open tourer is totally original including paint and leather. Being driven here by the American collector Peter Shumway, it is now in Berlin, Germany, in the Klaus Schildback collection.

The Zatuszek SSK owned by Brian Brunthorst in Milwaukee and the Trossi SSK now in the Tom Perkins collection in California are the only two true competition chassis still in existence. However, many other competition cars were converted for road use by the factory and still have racing engines. These engines use the large, eighteen-fin blower and a double oil pump; otherwise, they are the same as the standard production model.

If you cannot have originality, the next best thing is correctness. Considering today's value of S-series cars, it is highly unlikely that any additional cars will be converted to SSKs. However, existing cars will continually be improved with correct parts to the point where they will be almost indistinguishable from the original. Should a question of originality arise, Daimler-Benz has records of all chassis and engine numbers and the form in which they left the factory.

The SSK is without a doubt the rarest and most desirable sports Mercedes ever built. Its perfect blend of elegance and mechanical sophistication is approached by only two

A ride anyone? This German-owned SSK is absolutely correct in every detail and is the pride of its owner, Berthold Ruchwarth. This factory racing body was normally sold to the public with full fenders, rather than cycle fenders as shown here. One gets the feeling this car is almost all engine, with the rest of the car merely serving to carry and control the engine.

This SSK was originally owned by the Grand Prix driver Count Trossi. After its racing career, he rebodied it with this incredible Italian body. It is now in the Tom Perkins collection in California, where it has been brought back to original condition, both cosmetically and mechanically.

other vintage sports cars of the period: the type 55 Bugatti and the 2.9 Alfa Romeo.

SSKL, 1931-34

The 1930 racing season ended three years of competition for the SSK—a long time for any race car to remain competitive. However, the worldwide economic depression was strongly felt at Mercedes, and without development money, there was no chance of a totally new design from the racing department. Instead, the engineers set out to trim 250 pounds and add 50 hp to the existing SSK, creating the SSKL.

The most obvious lightening was to the chassis frame, which was drilled with holes along its entire length. Drilling holes was also done to the brake drums, pedals and anywhere else it could be used without destroying structural integrity. Wherever feasible, aluminum parts were replaced by magnesium.

To get the additional 50 hp, the compression was increased and a larger, eighteen-fin blower with a higher gear ratio (which could be engaged full time) was installed. Also, a hotter camshaft profile design was added, and a surprising feature, a totally new Scintilla ignition system, was installed (replacing the Bosch system used on standard S-series cars).

The SSKL was raced until 1933, when the newly designed W-25 ushered in a new era in Grand Prix racing.

Other than a powertrain found in Argentina, no SSKL is known to still exist. There have been rumors for years about a car in the Eastern Block. However, no hard evidence has surfaced. The SSKL was the end of the era when auto manufacturers offered their latest racing cars to the public as high-performance sports cars. From that point on, the division between production car design and racing machinery became very clearcut. The year 1933 brought the 380K for the sportsman, and the W-25 for the racing team.

This special SSK, bodied by Papler, is beautiful beyond words. It started its life as a race car, was then rebuilt by Mercedes and sent to Papler in Cologne for rebodying. Difficult to improve on this one! It was one of the few late-development S-series cars produced from 1930 to 1933.

The SSKL in full glory. Although holes appear only in the front and rear of this SSKL, the frame was lightened through its full length with covers placed over the center portions of the frame rails. If an example of this car were found, it would be the most valuable Mercedes-Benz in existence. To date, only pieces have been uncovered in Argentina.

Chapter 2

Prewar unsupercharged

Prewar Mercedes-Benzes (1926-40) are very popular collector cars. All of the supercharged models have been snapped up, but there are a surprising number of prewar unblown models still available. What is more surprising is that unblown models such as the 170, 230, 290, 320 and 380 can be had for a relatively low price. These unblown cars are very interesting for the buyer with limited funds but there are certain things you should know.

Should you decide you want one of these prewar models, keep in mind that these cars are a labor of love to restore, and in most cases their finished values do not financially justify a professional restoration. Parts can be difficult, if not impossible, to find. Explore these areas before you buy.

300, 320 and 350, 1926-34

The 300, 320, and 350 six-cylinder series' main attraction is historical, because these cars were a Ferdinand Porsche design. They featured very dependable, smooth running engines. However, some models were unexciting to drive, as the engine's power could not overcome the 6,000 pound weight of the car. The somewhat bland coachwork also detracted from these models.

1929: The best looking of the Stuttgart series, this 260 roadster was used in Alpine rallies. With 50 hp, up from 38 hp of the 200 Stuttgart, it was surprisingly nimble. (Mercedes-Benz)

★★★★	290 early cabriolet A (1933-34), 290 special roadster, 370K cabriolet A, 370K roadster, 370S cabriolet A, 370S roadster, 380S cabriolet A, 380S roadster
★★★	290, 230, 320 and 170 late cabriolet A (post-1935), 2-passenger cabriolet, roadster, 370K 4-passenger open body, 370S 4-passenger open body and 380S 4-passenger open body
★★	Open tourer, 290, 230, 320 and 170 4-passenger cabriolet, 370K closed car, 370S closed car, 380S closed car and other open cars
★	Sedan and other closed cars

200 and 260, 1929-38

The Stuttgart 200 and 260 models were much more exciting. Their ability to reach a top speed of 55 mph and their 6:1 rear gear ratio made them hot cars of the day. These cars were also the first Mercedes-Benzes to be fitted with a central lubrication system for chassis lubrication. This was a Mercedes feature on luxury models up through the end of 300d production in 1962. The cabriolets of this series are especially interesting but, unfortunately, very rare.

460 and 500, 1928-33

The Nurburg 460 and 500 models were very nice cars, featuring reasonable performance and some nice coachwork. They also had very smooth running engines and good braking. Their only mechanical downfall was a 5:1 rear axle ratio. This was necessary to make these 5,000 pound cars accelerate. The Nurburg models are very rare, but if you should consider one, choose a cabriolet or an open tourer.

The Nurburg was produced from 1929 to 1933. The same bodies were fitted to both models in 1931 and 1932. Total weights were approximately the same; the 20 additional horsepower of the 500 made it considerably sportier. The 460K ("K" for short chassis) on the left is very sporty and therefore desirable. The 500 on the right is a factory-bodied cabriolet F. (Mercedes-Benz)

350, 370, 370K, 370S and 380S, 1928-34

The Mannheim series was a particularly bright spot in prewar unblown production. The 370K and 370S six-cylinders and the 380S eight-cylinder are especially interesting. The cabriolet C, cabriolet A and roadster bodies are very beautiful, as they almost resemble a scaled-down SS car. They are also very rare.

170, 200, 230, 290 and 320, 1931-39

The six-cylinder 170, 200, 230, 290 and 320 were introduced throughout the 1930s.

TYPE: 370S

ENGINE
Type	6-cyl 3.7-ltr
Bore x stroke	82.5x115 mm
Displacement	3663 cc
Compression ratio	1:5.5
Horsepower	78 hp@3400 rpm

CHASSIS & DRIVETRAIN
Transmission	4-speed manual
Rear axle ratio	4.90

GENERAL
Wheelbase	2850 mm
Track, front and rear	1420 mm
Tire size, front and rear	5.50x18
Maximum speed	115 km/h
Fuel consumption	18.5 ltr/100 km
Gas tank capacity	70 ltr

TYPE: 230

ENGINE
Type	6-cyl 2.3-ltr
Bore x stroke	73.5x90 mm
Displacement	2289 cc
Compression ratio	1:6.6
Horsepower	55 hp@3500 rpm
Torque	14.0 mkg@1800 rpm

CHASSIS & DRIVETRAIN
Transmission	4-speed manual
Rear axle ratio	4.625

GENERAL
Wheelbase	3050 mm
Track, front/rear	1382/1412 mm
Tire size, front and rear	6.00x16
Weight	1900 kg, 1470 kg (limousine)
Maximum speed	116 km/h
Fuel consumption	16 ltr/100 km
Gas tank capacity	50 ltr

This beautifully restored 370S Mannheim is in the Mercedes-Benz factory museum in Stuttgart. The 370S is the most desirable of the unsupercharged cars of the thirties. Although its bodyline is extremely beautiful, the 370S cannot offer as much as the supercharged models in terms of mechanical desirability and will, therefore, never be as valuable. (Mercedes-Benz)

The 170 and 200 were inexpensive, small cars with about 32 hp. The only models in this group with much collector value are the sport roadsters and they will only appeal to the connoisseur of small cars. (Remember: The 170 is a six-cylinder, and the 170V and 170H had four-cylinder engines.)

In 1937, Mercedes introduced the 230, 290 and 320 models. These are of interest to collectors because there are still a number to be found. The 290 featured a new 60 hp engine and, in some cases, elegant coachwork. The cabriolet As and roadsters and a special roadster on a shortened 320 chassis are of special note. The coupe-roadster had a removable hardtop which continued into the postwar SL series.

TYPE: 320

ENGINE

Type	6-cyl 3.2-ltr
Bore x stroke	85x100 mm
Displacement	3405 cc
Compression ratio	1:6.25
Horsepower	78 hp@4000 rpm
Torque	22.2 mkg@1700 rpm

CHASSIS & DRIVETRAIN

Transmission	4-speed manual
Rear axle ratio	3.18

GENERAL

Wheelbase	3300 mm
Track, front/rear	1475/1500 mm
Tire size, front and rear	6.50x17
Weight	1950 kg
Maximum speed	126 km/h
Fuel consumption	18 ltr/100 km
Gas tank capacity	72 ltr

TYPE: 290

ENGINE

Type	6-cyl 2.9-ltr
Bore x stroke	78x100 mm
Displacement	2867 cc
Compression ratio	1:6.6
Horsepower	68 hp@3200 rpm

CHASSIS & DRIVETRAIN

Transmission	4-speed manual
Rear axle ratio	6.12

GENERAL

Wheelbase	3300 mm
Track, front/rear	1440/1476 mm
Tire size, front and rear	6.50x17
Weight	1850 kg
Maximum speed	103 km/h
Fuel consumption	17 ltr/100 km
Gas tank capacity	56 ltr

260D, 1936-40

The 260D is of historical interest since it was the first production diesel car, but it has very low performance and uninteresting coachwork.

130, 150, 170H and 170V, 1933-53

The rear-engined 130, 150 and 170H (predecessors to the Volkswagen) are interesting as novelties, but are very rare. The four-cylinder 170V was a small car like the 170 of the earlier six-cylinder series, with some interesting coachwork. Again, the cabriolet A and roadsters are of special note and are more collectible.

This prewar 230 cabriolet A shows the basic lines chosen by Mercedes for its postwar 170, 220 and 300 cabriolet models. (Alex Dearborn)

The 1938 320 cabriolet B was a popular car in the late thirties, with many examples still surviving.

The 1938 260D landaulette was the first diesel-powered production car, the predecessor to a large portion of Mercedes standard production sedans.

A pre-1940 170V roadster recently found in Poland. This is the most desirable configuration for this model. (Rainer Hitzbleck)

The top photograph is of a 170V cabriolet A;
below it is a cabriolet B. The A tops the B in
terms of investment value. (Rainer Hitzbleck)

Number of cylinders	4
Bore	73.5 mm
Stroke	100 mm
Cubic capacity	1697 ccm.
R.A.C. Rating	13.4 H.P.
Power developed	38 B.H.P.
Compression ratios available for ordinary petrol and for special fuels	
Firing order	1 3 4 2
Wheelbase	9 ft. 4 ins.
Track, in front	4 ft. 4 ins.
Track, at rear	4 ft. $3^1/_2$ ins.
Overall length	14 ft. 0 ins.
Overall width	5 ft. $1^3/_4$ ins.
Overall height (without passengers)	5 ft. $3^1/_4$ ins.
Ground clearance	8 ins.
Weight of chassis	appr. $12^3/_4$ cwt.
Weight of complete car	appr. $21^1/_2$ cwt.
Total reduction in 4th gear	1 : 4.1
Tyres	5.25 - 16
Maximum speed	appr. 75 m.p.h.
(under favourable conditions)	
Fuel consumption	appr. 30 m.p.g.
Oil consumption	appr. 2000 m.p.g.
Capacity of fuel tank $7^1/_4$ gallons including a reserve just over half a gallon	
Turning circle	36 ft.
Capacity of battery	74 amp./hrs.
Capacity of cooling system	2 gallons
Oil carried in crankcase	1 gallon

170V chassis: The very solid oval tubular chassis frame with independent suspension proved very durable, and continued with the development of the postwar 170, 220 and 300 series. (Adapted from the factory brochure.)

Chapter 3

Prewar eight-cylinder supercharged

380, 1933-34

The S series reached full development in 1932, and Mercedes began work on a supercharged replacement. Times were changing, and Mercedes felt the public wanted more comfortable and elaborately fitted cars. As a result, it introduced the model 380 (which is often unofficially referred to as the 380K, but not by the factory).

The 380 was a very nicely proportioned car and was offered in two-seater roadster, cabriolet A and coupe bodies along with four-passenger cabriolet B, cabriolet C and closed four-door sedan coachwork. All ver-

sions were powered by a 3.8 liter blown eight-cylinder engine.

Sometimes overlooked as a little sister of the 500 and 540K, the 380 is very interesting on its own merit and deserves as much attention as its two more famous brothers.

500K, 1934-36

The basic design of the 380's 120 hp engine was increased to five liters and it became the powerplant for the 500K. This,

This 380 cabriolet A is among the most beautiful of the eight-cylinder cars. Even without the much-desired external exhaust, its lines are clean and powerful. (Mercedes-Benz)

The 1932 sports roadster is a long-bodied roadster with the radiator and engine set forward. Compare it with the more pleasing short-bodied cabriolet A, which has perfect proportions. The 380 was also available with the short-bodied special roadster. (Mercedes-Benz)

☆☆☆★★	380, 500K, 540K, 580K special roadster
☆★★★★	380, 500K, 540K, 580K roadster, cabriolet A and tourer
★★★★★	380, 500K, 540K, 580K 2-passenger coupe and 770K
★★★★	380, 500K, 540K, 580K cabriolet B and C
★★★	380, 500K, 540K, 580K sedan

The 380: a Mercedes contradiction, clearly supercharged but clearly internally exhausted—no pipes. It is very possible that the last few 380s were externally exhausted, prototyping its successor, the 500K.

The earliest body type on a 500K chassis. This very sporty model featured cutaway doors, sidecurtains and a very round tail with a rumble seat. As with most two-seaters, the radiator and engine were moved back to shorten the cockpit. The special roadster, as opposed to the standard roadster, always used a v-shaped windshield. This basic body was first used on the supercharged 380. The main differences between them was that the 380 did not use the right-hand exterior exhaust and the shorter 380 wheelbase.

TYPE: 380	
ENGINE	
Type	8-cyl 3.8-ltr
Bore x stroke	78x100 mm
Displacement	3820 cc
Horsepower	120 hp@3400 rpm
CHASSIS & DRIVETRAIN	
Transmission	4-speed manual
Rear axle ratio	5.11
GENERAL	
Wheelbase	3140 mm
Track, front/rear	1435/1480 mm
Tire size, front and rear	6.50x17
Maximum speed	130 km/h
Fuel consumption	21 ltr/100 km
Gas tank capacity	90 ltr

along with a large blower, pushed the 500K's horsepower to 150. Eight bodies were offered on the 500K: standard roadster, special roadster, open tourer, cabriolet A, cabriolet B, cabriolet C, saloon and an aerodynamic coupe called an Autobahn Kurier.

Today more than ever, the value of an eight-cylinder supercharged car is drastically affected by the car's body type. A 500K special roadster, for example, is worth ten times as much as a five-passenger coupe or an unattractive convertible.

A 500K is a very valuable car on today's market. Remember, with all such cars, cor-

The standard roadster: Notice the flat windshield and the long cockpit, due to the engine and radiator being more forward. Other details are basically similar to the special roadster. (Alex Dearborn)

```
TYPE: 500K
ENGINE
Type  . . . . . . . . . . . . . . . . . . . . . . . . . .  8-cyl 5-ltr
Bore x stroke  . . . . . . . . . . . . . . . . . . . . .  86x108mm
Displacement  . . . . . . . . . . . . . . . . . . . . . . 5018 cc
Compression ratio . . . . . . . . . . . . . . . . . . . . . . 1:5.5
Horsepower  . . . . . . . . . . . . . . . 160 hp@3400 rpm
CHASSIS & DRIVETRAIN
Transmission  . . . . . . . . . . . . . . . . . . 4-speed manual
Rear axle ratio . . . . . . . . . . . . . . . . . . . . . . . . . 4.88
GENERAL
Wheelbase  . . . . . . . . . . . . . . . . . . . . . . . . 3290 mm
Track, front/rear . . . . . . . . . . . . . . . . . 1535/1547 mm
Tire size, front and rear  . . . . . . . . . . . . 7.50x17 extra
Weight . . . . . . . . . . . . . . . . . . . . . . . . . . . 2350 kg
Maximum speed  . . . . . . . . . . . . . . . . . . . . 160 km/h
Fuel consumption . . . . . . . . . . . . . . . . 27 ltr/100 km
Gas tank capacity  . . . . . . . . . . . . . . . . . . . . 110 ltr
```

rectness is more important than general condition. Arm yourself with an expert or good detail photos when considering the purchase of a 500K.

540K, 1936-39

The 540K continued the supercharged line with a 5.4 liter blown engine producing 180 hp. Although it had less horsepower than the S series of ten years earlier, many collectors prefer the 540K because of its looks. The 540K is a rare example of a model with body lines so striking that they outweigh engine power and thus performance

as the prime basis of value. This is particularly true of the special roadster which demands prices equal to the best S series cars. The body lines of the 540K were more rounded than those of the 500K and 380, a difference that people strongly like or dislike—strictly a matter of taste.

Since a special roadster is very valuable, use an expert's assistance to verify originality of the body. It is possible to rebody a less expensive cabriolet-B- or sedan-bodied car with a special roadster body. These rebodied cars are interesting, but not as valuable as originals.

```
TYPE: 540K
ENGINE
Type  . . . . . . . . . . . . . . . . . . . . . . . . .  8-cyl 5.4-ltr
Bore x stroke  . . . . . . . . . . . . . . . . . . . . .  88x111 mm
Displacement  . . . . . . . . . . . . . . . . . . . . . . 5401 cc
Compression ratio . . . . . . . . . . . . . . . . . . . . . . 1:5.2
Horsepower  . . . . . . . . . . . . . . . 180 hp@3400 rpm
Torque . . . . . . . . . . . . . . . . . . . . . 44 mkg@2200 rpm
CHASSIS & DRIVETRAIN
Transmission  . . . . . . . . . . . . . . . . 4- or 5-speed manual
Rear axle ratio . . . . . . . . . . . . . . . . 3.08, 3.60 or 3.50
GENERAL
Wheelbase  . . . . . . . . . . . . . . . . . . . . . . . . 3290 mm
Track, front/rear  . . . . . . . . . . . . . . . . 1535/1547 mm
Tire size, front and rear  . . . . . . . . . . . . 7.50x17 extra
Maximum speed  . . . . . . . . . . . . . . . . . . . . 170 km/h
Fuel consumption . . . . . . . . . . . . . . . . 29 ltr/100 km
Gas tank capacity  . . . . . . . . . . . . . . . . . . . . 110 ltr
```

This is basically a 500K special roadster modified to an elegant coupe. This one-of-a-kind factory-bodied car was originally owned by Rudolph Caracciola and is now in the hands of a lucky California collector.

770K, 1930-43

The 770K was built in two periods: the early series, 1930-38, and the late series, 1938-43. The early series, referred to by the factory as WO7, had small knock-off hubs; the late series had much larger knock-offs. The engines were basically the same, with engineering developments continuing through both periods.

TYPE: Early 770K
ENGINE
Type 8-cyl 7.7-ltr
Bore x stroke .... 95x135 mm
Displacement .... 7655 cc
Compression ratio 1:4.7
Horsepower .... 200 hp@2800 rpm
CHASSIS & DRIVETRAIN
Transmission .... 3-speed manual
Rear axle ratio .... 4.50 or 4.88
GENERAL
Wheelbase .... 3750 mm
Track, front and rear .... 1500 mm
Tire size, front and rear 7.00x20
Weight .... 2700 kg
Maximum speed .... 160 km/h
Fuel consumption .... 30 ltr/100 km
Gas tank capacity .... 120 ltr

TYPE: LATE 770K
ENGINE
Type 8-cyl 7.7-ltr
Bore x stroke .... 95x135 mm
Displacement .... 7655 cc
Compression ratio 1:7.2
Horsepower .... 230 hp@3200 rpm
CHASSIS & DRIVETRAIN
Transmission .... 5-speed manual
Rear axle ratio 4.11
GENERAL
Wheelbase .... 3880 mm
Track, front/rear .... 1600/1650 mm
Tire size, front and rear 8.25x19
Weight .... 4780 kg
Maximum speed .... 180 km/h
Fuel consumption .... 38 ltr/100 km
Gas tank capacity .... 300 ltr

The early models were built mostly for the public and private use of heads of state. The later models were produced for the official use of the government, especially the Third Reich.

These cars are rarely for sale. When one does surface, it is usually purchased by a museum.

This 540K coupe, although closed, is a very beautiful car. Its stunning line along with its rarity make it close in value to the cabriolet A.

This particular car was also first owned by the famous Mercedes driver Rudolph Caracciola.

The rarest development of the early 380, 500K, and 540 special roadster. The cutaway doors and v-windshield were preserved. However, the rear deck was tapered rather than rounded as on the early 380/500K special roadsters.

More sleekness but less sportiness. This body has roll-up windows and more taper to the rear. This model is considered by many enthusiasts to be the most desirable of the prewar eight-cylinder supercharged cars.

The last development of the special roadster was the 540K. It has grown close in appearance to the 540K cabriolet A, but with the disappearing top. Relatively speaking, it lacks sportiness and sleekness when compared to its predecessor. It, therefore, does not command the same value.

This 540K cabriolet A with rear-mounted spares is generally more sporty than its side-mounted-spare sibling. However, spare location is often a personal preference, and does not affect values in most cases.

Chapter 4

Postwar four-cylinder

170V, 1946-53

The four-cylinder 170V was first introduced at the Berlin Auto Show in 1936. (The discussion goes on to this day as to whether the V stands for the German word *vergaser* meaning carbureted or the word *vorn* meaning front. It's become a matter of opinion among the experts.) During the war, Mercedes was eighty percent destroyed. After the war, the company was left with outdated equipment and prewar parts, so the most practical approach was to build from existing engineering and materials, which Mercedes did. It reintroduced the 170V, in its original form, in 1946.

The 170V developed into the 170Va and 170Vb during its eight-year production run. The Va, introduced in 1950, had a slightly larger engine with seven more horsepower, and improved suspension. In 1952, the Vb made its debut, featuring minor mechanical and body changes including a larger windshield and a new rear axle design.

Although the 170V, with its suicide doors, running boards, unmistakable grille and external headlights, might fit the definition of a classic car, it probably belongs in the "cute"

category instead. The 170V also has two advantages: One, it saw fewer years of use

```
TYPE: 170V
ENGINE
Type ......................... 4-cyl (M 136)
Bore x stroke ............. 73.5x100 mm (2.89x3.94 in)
Displacement ............................. 1697 cc
Valve operation ......... single overhead cam, chain driven
Compression ratio ............................. 6:1
Fuel system ......... 1 updraft carburetor Solex 30 BFLVS
Horsepower ................. 38 hp (DIN) @3600 rpm
Torque ................. 10 mkg@1800 rpm (72.35 ft/lb)
CHASSIS & DRIVETRAIN
Clutch ......................... single dry-plate
Transmission ..................... 4-speed manual
Rear suspension ............... swing axle, coil springs
Rear axle ratio ............................. 4.125:1
Front suspension ..................... independent
Frame ................. x-shaped oval tubular
GENERAL
Wheelbase ..................... 2845 mm (112 in)
Track, front/rear ........... 1310/1296 mm (51.6/51.0 in)
Brakes ......................... drum
Steering ratio ............................. 14.4:1
Wheels ......................... 16 in steel disc
Tire size, front and rear ..................... 5.50x16
Weight ......................... 1160 kg (2552 lb)
Maximum speed ..................... 108 km/h (67 mph)
Acceleration ..................... 36 sec 0-100 km
Fuel consumption ................. 11 ltr/100 km (21 mpg)
Gas tank capacity ..................... 42 ltr (11.1 gal)
```

★★★   **170S and 170V roadster, 170S and 170V cabriolet A, 190SL coupe and 190SL roadster**
★★   **Offen touringwagen-Polizei**
★   **All sedans, 180, 190, 200**

than the average car of the thirties and, two, it benefited from some postwar engineering.

The prewar 170V was available in roadster, cabriolet B, cabriolet A, Offen touren-wagen-Polizei (police open tourer wagon) and sedan form. Unfortunately, the postwar V, Va and Vb were produced only in four-door sedan and commercial versions.

Although the mechanics of the 170 are historically interesting, it is a simple design and lacks mechanical sophistication. Therefore, it will never achieve the kind of prices demanded by its bigger brothers.

If your interest is primarily enjoyment of ownership, the 170V is worth consideration. In good condition, these cars are very drivable, and they have passed the test of time in terms of reliability. The inexpensive nature of the cars translates into reasonably priced spare parts.

As a general rule, the lower the value of the car, the more you should be concerned with its condition. The most important points when examining a 170V are the parts most expensive to restore. Generally check the main body structure for rust, test the sound-ness of plated parts and examine the condition of the interior. Again, the overall completeness and originality of the car are also factors. Remember that restoration of mechanical parts is usually more affordable than major body or interior work. Always check the condition of rubber brake lines and the central lubrication system.

Should you find a prewar 170V cabriolet A or roadster, and the price is right, make sure you check all wooden frame parts for rot, as they are very expensive to replace.

170S, 1949-55

In 1949 the 170S was introduced as an extension of the 170V series. During its production run from 1949 to 1955 it, like the V, evolved into two models: the 170Sb and 170S-V. The 170S (special) developed from the 170V, with the greatest difference being the introduction of the Solex downdraft carburetor. The basic chassis design was also improved by increasing the front and rear tracks and improving the suspension. The body size was increased, but the 170S still retained the classic prewar lines of the 170V.

The 170Va used vertical louvers on the side hood panel, as opposed to horizontal louvers on the 170Vb. An option on this 170 was the addition of the glass windproofing attachment to the front door windows. The 170Va and Vb were also available in a two-door sedan and cabriolet sedan with slide-down top similar to a full sunroof over the front and rear seat. Note spare tire mount on trunk. (Mercedes-Benz)

The 170Sb, introduced in 1952, saw the gearshift lever moved to the steering column, an improved heater and a hand-activated starter button on the dash rather than a foot-activated starter button on the floor.

The 170S-V, making its debut in mid-1953, closed out the series as a combination of all its predecessors. The S-V used the engine and front axle from the 170V, the chassis of the Sb and body of the S.

The 170S was available as a four-door sedan; a two-door, five-passenger cabriolet B; and a two-door, two- or three-passenger cabriolet A.

In terms of value, the very sporty two-door cabriolet A is most desirable, followed by the two-door cabriolet B, with the four-door sedan on the bottom. Your choice between the 170S and 170V can be made primarily by taste. Of course, any prewar model demands a higher price.

When examining the 170S, keep in mind all the considerations for the 170V, as they are the same concerns.

TYPE: 170S/170Sb

ENGINE
Type . . . . 4-cyl (M 136)
Bore x stroke . . . . 75x100 mm (2.95x3.94 in)
Displacement . . . . 1767 cc (107.7 cu in)
Valve operation . . . . single overhead cam, chain driven
Compression ratio 6.5:1
Fuel system . . . . 1 downdraft carburetor Solex 32 PBJ
Horsepower . . . . 52 hp (DIN) @4000 rpm
Torque . . . . 11.4 mkg@1800 rpm (82.5 ft/lb)

CHASSIS & DRIVETRAIN
Clutch . . . . single dry-plate
Transmission . . . . 4-speed manual
Rear suspension . . . . swing axle, with coil springs
Rear axle ratio . . . . S: 4.375:1, Sb: 4.44:1
Front suspension . . . . independent
Frame . . . . x-shaped oval tubular

GENERAL
Wheelbase . . . . 2845 mm (112 in)
Track, front/rear . . . . S: 1315/1420 mm (51.57/55.89 in);
   Sb: 1315/1435 mm (51.57/56.49 in)
Brakes . . . . drum
Steering ratio 13.9:1
Wheels . . . . 15 in steel disc
Tire size, front and rear 6.40x15
Weight . . . . S: 1220 kg (2684 lb); Sb: 1250 kg (2750 lbs)
Maximum speed . . . . 122 km/h (76 mph)
Acceleration . . . . 32 sec 0-100 km
Fuel consumption . . . . 12 ltr/100 km (19.5 mpg)
Gas tank capacity . . . . 47 ltr (12.4 gal)

The 170 open touring police car used a very sporty fold-down windscreen and quite attractive open touring body. With painted rather than plated brightwork, this model was obviously used for military purposes. (Mercedes-Benz)

The standard 170S sedan had a slightly modernized roofline compared with the 170V. Also, the spare tire has been moved inside the trunk. The 170S represents the first really new postwar Mercedes, with the 170V being both a prewar and a postwar car. (Mercedes-Benz)

The 170S cabriolet B, unlike the 170S cabriolet A, used a metal rather than wood body frame—a big help for the restorer. The radiator ornament was truly functional as a radiator cap. The 170S is the last model for which this can be said. Notice the Sindelfingen coachbuilding tag at the lower front corner of the door. This, as with prewar cars, indicates a factory body. (Mercedes-Benz)

180, 190 and 200, 1953-68

In 1953 Mercedes-Benz introduced a radically new car: the 180. This car used the same engine as the 170S but featured a totally new concept in chassis and body design, referred to as unibody construction. The chassis frame was replaced by a steel inner-body structure with the front axle and motor forming a detachable subframe, easily removed for service.

These new engineering designs make the 180 technically and historically interesting. However, because it was offered only as a sedan, it will never have strong collectibility.

Also using this same unibody construction was the 190, introduced in 1956. The 190 featured a new four-cylinder overhead cam engine with an aluminum head and a cast-iron block. This new motor boasted 80 hp, up from the 180's 68 hp.

The 190b bowed in 1959 with a modernized body, a wider radiator shell and a higher-compression engine that bumped the horsepower up five.

Another new body was introduced in 1961 for the 190c. The new model continued to use the 190b engine but had a body very similar to the fin-back 220Sb body introduced in 1959. The 190c was shorter than the 220Sb and had different front fenders, identifiable by the single headlight as opposed to the 220Sb's double headlights.

The 200 was based on the 190c body and the 190 four-cylinder engine, but it featured a few improvements. Displacement was increased to two liters, plus two carburetors and higher compression boosted the motor to 95 hp. The body was still offered only in a sedan version.

The 180, 190 and 200 models are not likely to be good investments, but they can be enjoyable transportation should you find one in good condition.

190SL, 1955-63

Another Mercedes-Benz sports car went into production in 1955: the 190SL. This car was designed as a scaled-down unibody ver-

Visually similar to the 300SL roadster, the 190SL was less than half the price when new and less than one-fifth the price today. This pair shows the variety possible with a removable hardtop. (Mercedes-Benz)

sion of the 300SL. The 190SL was smaller not only in size but also in performance, mechanical sophistication and price. At less than half the price of the 300SL, the 190SL was aimed at a market more interested in elegant sports touring than high performance.

Comparisons aside, the 190SL was a very attractive sports car, easily able to stand on its own merit. The car used a punched-up version of the standard 52 hp 180 engine. Two horizontally mounted two-barrel Solex carburetors and hotter compression put the 190SL engine at 105 hp. The 190SL could attain a top speed of 106 mph and go 0-60 mph in twelve to thirteen seconds. Another interesting feature of the 190SL was its unibody design: mounting the engine and front axle on a subframe which could easily be detached and rolled away from the main body section. The remainder of the body and chassis used the standard unibody construction.

Sales literature of the era describes both a coupe and a roadster version of the 190SL, but the two were basically the same car. The hardtop was optional on the roadster (which came with the soft top) and the soft top was an option on the coupe (which had the detachable hardtop).

Independent front and rear suspension made both roadholding and comfort excellent. The vacuum servo-assist drum brakes made braking this light car effortless. The 190SL, like the 300SL, was equipped with an ATE T-50 vacuum brake booster, which can develop leaks with age, but rebuild kits are available through aftermarket suppliers.

Although the 190SL was quite small, it was roomy with two bucket-style seats, a storage area behind the seats and a fairly roomy trunk. Leather upholstery, fitted luggage and a rear jump seat were options. The only drawback to good all-weather usage, provided the optional hardtop was in place, was an inadequate heater. The alumi-

Skis point out the all-weather nature of the SL. Factory-designed ski rack allowed access to the trunk with skis in place. This is an early version, with small rear taillights. In 1956 a larger version of this light was fitted. The 190SL is perfect for a weekend trip in the country, with comfortable bucket seats, good fuel economy, fitted luggage and simple mechanical maintenance (except for carburetors). Powerwise, remember it is only a 1.9 liter four-cylinder. (Mercedes-Benz)

num doors, trunk and hood put the 190SL at 2,550 pounds.

During its eight years of production, the 190SL went through several minor modifications, including some body changes. The most obvious body changes were the addition of chrome trim in 1956, the relocation of the license plate lights from the body to the bumper guards in 1957, and a dash clock in 1957.

Mechanical changes included new brake cylinders and various rear axle ratios. Many cars have been converted to Weber, Stromberg and even SU carburetors. Some claim the original Solex carbs can be tuned properly with a little extra effort, and if you intend to show the car they do maintain originality. When examining the car, make sure the brace below the carburetors is firmly in place. (Amateur mechanics often fail to reconnect this bracket because of the difficulty involved.) Remember that these cars have only three main bearings and do not take kindly to abuse or power-increasing modifications. As is generally true with all

series, the later-model 190SLs are a bit more desirable because of minor engineering improvements.

The 190SL is a good choice for the sports car enthusiast with limited funds and limited

TYPE: 190SL	
ENGINE	
Type	4-cyl (M 121)
Bore x stroke	85x83.6 mm (3.35x3.29 in)
Displacement	1897 cc (115.7 cu in)
Valve operation	single overhead cam, chain driven
Compression ratio	8.5:1
Fuel system	2 dual downdraft carburetors, Solex 44 PHH
Horsepower	105 hp (DIN) @5700 rpm
Torque	14.5 mkg@3200 rpm (105 ft/lb@ 3200 rpm)
CHASSIS & DRIVETRAIN	
Clutch	single dry-plate
Transmission	4-speed manual
Rear suspension	single joint swing axle, coil springs
Rear axle ratio	3.90 (39:10)
Front suspension	independent
Frame	unit frame and body
GENERAL	
Wheelbase	2400 mm (94.5 in)
Track, front/rear	1430/1475 mm (56.2/58.1 in)
Brakes	drum
Steering ratio	18.5:1
Wheels	13 in steel disc
Tire size, front and rear	6.40x13 sport
Weight	1180 kg (2596 lb) with hardtop
Maximum speed	171 km/h (106 mph)
Acceleration	14.5 sec 0-100 km
Fuel consumption	12.5 ltr super/100 km (18.75 mpg)
Gas tank capacity	65 ltr (17 gal)

The 190SL interior with the third seat a transverse rear seat. (Alex Dearborn)

The engine space of the 190SL, showing the large two-barrel Solex carburetors and air induction tube. (Alex Dearborn)

facilities for undertaking complicated mechanical service. Other than the tricky tuning adjustments of the Solex carburetors, the 190SL is very easy to maintain. You may find that several engine components have been modified. Some of the more obvious ones include engine mounts, air filters, oil filters, water pumps, wrist pins, valve covers and ignition systems.

As with many unibody cars, the 190SL is very susceptible to rust which, if serious, can destroy the structural strength of the entire chassis. In particular, check the attachment of the rear axle follower arms to the body. These have been known to come loose during driving, which can be very dangerous.

One other point to check is the jack mounts built into the unibody. Corrosion weakens these, leaving no way to lift the car with a factory jack. One sure way to tell if any bodywork has been done is to check the rocker panels at the rear of the doors. You should see vertical seams; if you don't, these may have been covered up in rust repair.

The 190SL, with its sporty and appealing coupe-roadster body, will always be a very sought after collector item. Using recent records as a guide, the 190SL is second only to the 300SL in desirability, and it is mechanically simpler. Although they lack performance, 190SLs are quite plentiful and inexpensive to buy and restore.

Original options included a hardtop (now hard to find) and fitted luggage (extremely rare). Two different hardtops were made, one with a small window (1955-59), the other with a larger window (1959-63).

190SL production ended in February 1963 with only 104 cars built the final year. If you are considering a "1963" car, be sure to verify the year by the chassis number. Some cars built in late 1962 were sold and titled as 1963s, and owners sometimes think that 1963 on the title makes the car worth more.

The unibody 190SL chassis had solid-box-type sections which formed the backbone of the frame floor unit. This design allowed for more energy absorption in a crash than the conventional solid chassis frame with separate body.

Chapter 5

Early postwar six-cylinder

220, 1951-60

Introduced in 1951, the 220 was the first production Mercedes-Benz to incorporate the headlights into the front fenders. Other than this little touch of modernization, the 220 body was basically the same as the 170. Mechanically, however, the 220 was an innovative new car and a real trendsetter. Its reliable 2.2 liter six-cylinder iron-block aluminum-head single overhead cam engine survived basically unchanged in newer models through 1972. This design proved so successful that it was used in all of the 220, 230 and 250 models. In fact, the entire 300 series, including the 300SL gullwing, shares the basic engine design of the modest 220.

The wide range of bodies in the 220 series has something for almost everyone. The four-door sedan may not have a great deal of investment value but it does have heart. Its ease of maintenance, drivability, classic lines and broad public appeal can start a lifelong Mercedes love affair.

The rarity of the cabriolet B, a two-door, five-passenger convertible, gives it good investment potential. The two-passenger coupe and cabriolet A, with their rarity and striking lines, are the most valuable of the early 220 series and are the models most likely to have the greatest investment potential.

The normal but very attractive sedan combined prewar styling with postwar technology at a very affordable price but without high appreciation potential. It had features such as fully reclining front seats and a locking steering wheel. (Mercedes-Benz)

★★★★	220 coupe, 220 cabriolet A, 220S cabriolet A and 220SE cabriolet A
★★★	220 cabriolet B, 220S coupe and 220SE coupe
★★	220 sedan, 220S and 220SE sedan
★	220a and 219

The 220, like the 170, used a tubular steel chassis with four-wheel independent suspension. The chassis was lubricated by a central lubricating system actuated by a foot pump located to the left of the clutch. The pump should be operated religiously every 200 miles, and it works beautifully when in good operating condition. The small lines,

Late 220 cabriolet A with one difference from early models: a curved rather than flat windshield. This model is the most desirable of 220 cabriolet As. (Mercedes-Benz)

Pictured here is the model cabriolet A, the most desirable of the 220 series. Notice the classic prewar body styling with the modern addition of integrated headlights. The 220 is also the first model to use the radiator shell more for decoration than function. (Alex Dearborn)

Very inviting with full touring trim, the trunk contained three-piece fitted luggage (optional), spare tire, jack and tools. Fitted luggage is a very desirable addition to any collectible Mercedes. (Alex Dearborn)

however, are vulnerable to blockage and should be checked frequently; otherwise, joints may starve for lubrication and wear quickly.

Examine the rubber boots covering the axle swing joints. These are susceptible to rot and very difficult to change. All rubber parts on Mercedes-Benzes of this vintage should be carefully examined for deterioration, especially brake lines and brake cylinder rubber. If your prospective car has been in storage for many years, just topping off

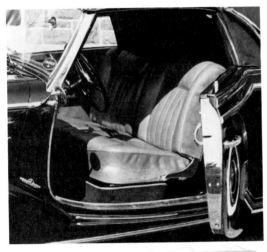

The interior of the 220 cabriolet A, as with other members of the 220 series, was very elegantly fitted with large bucket seats, wool carpeting and chrome doorjam covers. Notice in the left-hand corner of the photo, the Sindelfingen body tag. (Alex Dearborn)

This factory photo shows the interior of the 220 series, with large clock and speedometer. Dash and door trim are of veneered wood. (Alex Dearborn)

This very interesting photo shows a 1952 220 cabriolet A engine fitted with a 1965 220b short-block. This retrofit exchangeability is quite common with Mercedes and very important for the restorer. (Paul Russell)

The cabriolet top's thick horsehair lining was used by Mercedes on all of the cabriolet tops made for the all-weathertight nature of these cars.

Heating and ventilation

The Convertible "A" has a better air-conditioning-system than can be found in most homes. Fresh air is pressed in through a large scoop in the back of the grille while driving fast, respectively drawn in by a ventilator when the car is parked or being operated in dense traffic. The air is led into a preheating chamber where it is heated to the desired temperature by a warm-water heat exchanger. The heated air passes into the distribution chamber where it enters ducts leading to the side windows, windshield and interior. The temperature is regulated by means of a control on the instrument panel. The same

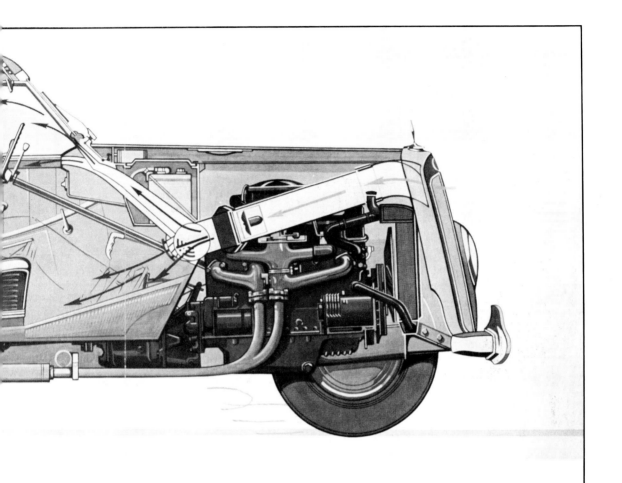

system without heating can be turned on in summer for the draft-free intake of cool, fresh air to add to your driving comfort.

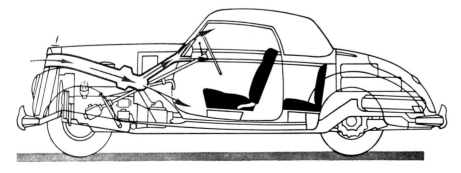

When in place, the auxiliary seat offers comfortable and spacious seating for two more persons.

the brake fluid may get the system working, but when you least expect it you may have total brake failure.

TYPE: 220	
ENGINE	
Type	6-cyl overhead camshaft (M180)
Bore x stroke	80x72.8 mm (3.15x2.87 in)
Displacement	2195 cc (133.9 cu in)
Valve operation	single overhead cam, chain driven
Compression ratio	6.5:1
Fuel system	1 dual downdraft carburetor, Solex 30 PAAJ
Horsepower	80 hp (DIN) @4850 rpm
Torque	14.5 mkg@2500 rpm (104.9 ft/lb)
CHASSIS & DRIVETRAIN	
Clutch	single dry-plate
Transmission	4-speed manual
Rear suspension	swing axle, coil springs
Rear axle ratio	4.44
Front suspension	independent
Frame	x-shaped oval tubular
GENERAL	
Wheelbase	2845 mm (112 in)
Track, front/rear	1315/1435 mm (51.6/56.5 in)
Brakes	drum
Steering ratio	13.9:1
Wheels	15 in steel disc
Tire size, front and rear	6.40x15
Weight	1350 kg (2970 lb); convertible, 1440 kg (3168 lb)
Maximum speed	141 km/h (87.5 mph); convertible B, 140 km/h; convertible A, 145 km/h
Fuel consumption	14 ltr/100 km (16.75 mpg); convertible A and B, 14.5 ltr
Gas tank capacity	65 ltr (17.2 gal)

The extremely rare two-door coupe used the same body as the cabriolet A with a fixed hard-top. Notice the prewar suicide doors. The jack mounts which appear below the running board molding front and rear are attached to the chassis frame and therefore cause very few problems compared with the later 220S with unibody construction, which rusts badly preventing their use. (Alex Dearborn)

Because the 220 used a solid chassis frame it is not as susceptible to structural rot as the unibody cars. Carefully check the tubular support body channels running from the firewall to the rear of the body. These often rust badly, and they are needed to support the body on the frame.

When the 220 cabriolet A was introduced, it was a deluxe model by comparison with other postwar Mercedes-Benzes. The cabriolet was updated in 1954 with the appearance of a coupe, and production continued into late 1955. You may see a car described as a 220a cabriolet, but no such model exists. These are often mistakenly used to describe a 220 cabriolet A. The later 220a, made from 1954 on, was the immediate precursor of the fin-back 220b (1959-65).

Special attention must be given to the condition of the cabriolet A's wooden body frame. The wood is expensive to replace and its condition affects the operation of the doors and top.

Mechanical parts for the 220 are not a great problem. Many are available from Mercedes-Benz and aftermarket specialists. Many parts, especially engine parts, are interchangeable with later models. The major exception is electrical parts, which are 6-volt on the early 220 and 12-volt on later cars.

The 220 series is a very good first venture into Mercedes collectibles. These cars are

Notice the optional exterior spare-tire mounting, allowing for more trunk room. As in most cases, the full-size rear seat detracts from the elegance of body styling and, therefore, collector value. (Alex Dearborn)

quiet, comfortable, very reliable and relatively simple and inexpensive to maintain—a pleasant blend of prewar styling and postwar engineering.

220S and 220SE, 1956-61

In 1956 the 220S was introduced as a direct descendant of the 220, although the body and chassis had undergone major changes. Unibody construction did away with the traditional tubular chassis frame of the earlier model 220.

The body was also substantially updated as the company (DBAG) eliminated running boards and reduced the prominence of the hood. After two years of production, a Bosch fuel-injection system was added to the basic 220S engine creating the 220SE. This not only added 15 hp but also increased engine reliability. Although the 220S engine varied slightly from its predecessor, parts are basically interchangeable. Mercedes listed the 220S and 220Sb engine blocks as replacements for the 220 engine, requiring only a

TYPE: 220S

ENGINE

Type	6-cyl overhead camshaft (M 180)
Bore x stroke	80x72.8 mm (3.16x2.87 in)
Displacement	2195 cc (133.9 cu in)
Valve operation	single overhead cam, chain driven
Compression ratio	8.7:1
Fuel system	2 dual downdraft carbs, Solex 34 PAJTA
Horsepower	110 hp (DIN) @5000 rpm
Torque	17.5 kmg@3500 rpm

CHASSIS & DRIVETRAIN

Clutch	single dry-plate
Transmission	4-speed manual & automatic
Rear suspension	single joint swing axle, coil springs
Rear axle ratio	3.90; automatic, 4.10
Front suspension	independent
Frame	unit frame and body

GENERAL

Wheelbase	2750 mm (108.3 in)
Track, front/rear	1470/1485 mm (57.9/58.5 in)
Brakes	drum
Steering ratio	21.4:1
Wheels	13 in steel disc
Tire size, front and rear	6.70x13 sport
Weight	1345 kg (2959 lb)
Maximum speed	165 km/h (103 mph)
Acceleration	15 sec 0-100 km/h
Fuel consumption	14 ltr, super/100 km (16.75 mpg); automatic: 15 ltr, super 100 km/h (15.6 mpg)
Gas tank capacity	65 ltr (17.2 gal)

Very attractive with the top down, this cabriolet A breaks the long tradition of landau irons. The white walls were probably an American consideration. (Mercedes-Benz)

simple modification to the engine mounts. Manifolds were also readily exchanged, but interchangeability was limited to the engine and some transmissions.

Retrofit provisions can be found throughout Mercedes' production, and it points out an interesting philosophy of Mercedes-Benz development. Once Mercedes developed a good product, it maintained it for a long time, only fine tuning it as newer technology became available. This technique probably has a lot to do with Mercedes-Benz' reputation as the best-engineered car in the world.

The 220S front axle and engine are detachable from the unibody, as opposed to the traditional design of the earlier model 220. The rear axle retains the independent suspension.

Where collectibility is concerned, the 220S and 220SE coupe and convertible stand far above the four-door sedan. In my opinion, these cars exhibit an unsurpassed level of elegance in postwar cars. It should be noted that the addition of fuel injection to the 220SE model increased its level of mechanical sophistication and, thereby, its value.

As with most vintage cars, the two-door convertible will usually demand a higher price than the two-door coupe, even though the latter is much more rare. Ironically though, the 220SE sedan, produced only as a 1959 model, is more rare than the convertible or the cabriolet.

When examining one of these cars, special attention must be paid to the numerous chrome moldings which are very fragile and expensive to replace. On some coupes with the rare two-tone paint option, a small chrome strip, now incredibly difficult to find, separates the two colors just behind the headlights.

Unlike the 220 cabriolet A, the 220S and 220SE cabriolet did not use a wooden body framework. This is a big plus in terms of

220SE cabriolet A looked more like a roadster than the traditional cabriolet A. Available in solid or two-tone paint. (Mercedes-Benz)

restoration. Since these models used uni-body construction, pay careful attention to rust in the structural body members.

The 1957-60 220S and 220SE had vacuum brake boosters similar to those of the 190SL and 300SL models. These tend to develop leaks, but rebuild kits are available.

Most of these cars have a fair amount of interior wood trim, which is vulnerable to the harmful effects of sunlight, water and wear. The original lacquer finish on the wood may have been removed and replaced by any of a number of other processes like polyurethane, varnish and so on. If the car's wood is veneer-covered, sanding has probably ruined the thin veneer. Reveneering and restoring the original lacquer can be done well, but will require an expert.

220S and 220SE: Definitely postwar in its body styling, notice the low hoodline, integrated front and rear fenders, smaller wheels and curved windshield. Also interesting is the absence of landau irons, allowing the top to store more compactly than in its predecessor, the 220A. (Alex Dearborn)

220S and SE cabriolet A: Although the chrome creates beautiful accent, it can be a great problem for the restorer. Particularly significant to early Mercedes is the compactness of the lowered convertible top. (Alex Dearborn)

220S and SE coupe. With elegance to spare, this all-weather coupe combined both a sense of formal sophistication with sportiness. Restoration is often easier on a coupe than a convertible because of less weather exposure and the cost of convertible top restoration. (Mercedes-Benz)

Engines are usually in need of overhaul at 100,000 miles, with valve guide wear being the most common ailment. Other parts such as water pumps, exhaust system components and motor mounts need occasional replacement. The 220's aluminum head was

Although the dash on this 220SE convertible appears to be solid burl, it is actually a beautiful job of veneering. Much skill and patience is required when restoring such woodwork.

TYPE: 220SE

ENGINE

Type	6-cyl overhead camshaft (M 180)
Bore x stroke,	80x72.8 mm (3.15x2.87 in)
Displacement	2195 cc (133.9 cu in)
Valve operation	single overhead cam, chain driven
Compression ratio	8.7:1
Fuel system	Bosch two-plunger pump
Horsepower	115 hp (DIN) @4800 rpm
Torque	19 mkg@3800 rpm

CHASSIS & DRIVETRAIN

Clutch	single dry-plate
Transmission	4-speed manual
Rear suspension	single joint swing axle, coil springs
Rear axle ratio	4.10
Front suspension	independent
Frame	unit frame and body

GENERAL

Wheelbase	2820 mm (111 in); coupe and convertible, 2700 mm (106.3 in)
Track, front and rear	1430/1470 mm (56.2/57.9 in)
Brakes	drum
Steering ratio	21.4:1
Wheels	13 in steel disc
Tire size, front and rear	6.70x13 sport
Weight	1370 kg (3014 lb); coupe, 1430 kg (3146 lb); convertible, 1470 kg (3234 lb)
Maximum speed	160 km/h (99.5 mph)
Acceleration	15 sec 0-100 km
Fuel consumption	13 ltr, super/100 km (18 mpg); coupe and convertible, 13.5 ltr (17.4 mpg)
Gas tank capacity	62 ltr (16.4 gal)

Although quite attractive and dependable, the 220 sedan can be purchased at a reasonable price, but condition is extremely important due to the fact that it is more expensive to restore one of these cars than it is worth in restored condition. (Alex Dearborn)

and still is susceptible to corrosion. Improper coolant can cause serious damage resulting in low compression, coolant in the cylinders and so on. Mercedes-Benz sells its own antifreeze, or you can use Prestone; but the important thing to remember is that the coolant must be replaced regularly to renew the anticorrosion additives. Fortunately, used heads are not difficult to find. An additional problem is that the small heater cores and small blower fans were effective only in mildly cold weather.

220 availability in descending order of rarity: two-door coupe, two-door cabriolet B, two-door cabriolet A, four-door sedan with sunroof, four-door sedan.

Market value in descending order of expense: cabriolet A, coupe, cabriolet B, sedan with sunroof, sedan.

The less-than-roomy rear seat of the 220S/SE coupe or cabriolet A converted into a much more usable luggage compartment, by rearrangement of seat cushions (Mercedes-Benz)

As on the 220, large bucket seats, wool carpeting, wood trim and chrome molding are standard. One point of particular interest on almost all Mercedes is that, although solid in appearance, the woodwork is veneered. This technique was not used to save money on wood but to allow for a construction technique of laminated sections which would avoid warping and cracking. An added benefit of this technique is more controllable visual effect of the woodgrain. Restoration of this woodwork is a challenge, even to a professional. (Alex Dearborn)

Chapter 6

300 series

The formidable 300 series contained the 300, 300b, 300c and 300d (the luxury limousines of the 1950s); the 300S and 300SC (the grand sports cars of the line); the 300SE and 300SEL (the fuel-injected version of the

The 300 cabriolet D was the last of the true full-sized four-passenger convertibles made by Mercedes. No doubt, the end of an era.

1960s); and the famous 300SL gullwing coupe and roadster.

The 300 series represented the upper level of DBAG's offerings, giving the collector a sense of grandness plus a sporty, sophisticated mechanical design. The series made its debut in 1951 with the 300 sedan, which developed through versions b, c and d, with production ending in 1962.

The 300S and fuel-injected 300Sc represented the returning influence of the grand sports tourer of the 1930s in its greatest form—sophisticated mechanics with beautifully proportioned lines.

Before World War II Daimler-Benz was renowned for building luxury cars, and the postwar 300 series marked its return to luxury car production. These cars exhibited a prewar styling influence yet included some of the most sophisticated engines and drivetrains ever seen in production cars.

☆★★★★	300SL gullwing coupe and 300Sc roadster
★★★★★	300S roadster, 300Sc cabriolet, 300SL coupe-roadster
★★★★	300 4-door convertible, 300S coupe, 300S cabriolet, 300Sc coupe and 300SE cabriolet
★★★	300SE coupe, 300b sedan, 300c sedan, 300d sedan and 300SEL sedan
★★	300 sedan

300, 300b, 300c and 300d, 1951-62

As with other Mercedes models, the designations b, c and d represented modifications to the original model. Detailing all of these changes is well beyond the scope of this book. However, in general, modifications b and c were mechanical in nature, and modification d represented modernization of the body and the addition of fuel injection.

The convertible versions offer a more desirable body type and therefore demand higher prices. All 300 models, both sedan and convertible, were expensive when new.

TYPE: 300	
ENGINE	
Type	6-cyl overhead camshaft (M 186)
Bore x stroke	85x88 mm (3.35x3.46 in)
Displacement	2996 cc (182.7 cu in)
Value operation	single overhead cam, chain driven
Compression ratio	6.4:1
Fuel system	2 dual downdraft carbs, Solex 40 PBJC
Horsepower	115 hp (DIN) @4600 rpm
Torque	20 mkg@2500 rpm (114 ft/lb)
CHASSIS & DRIVETRAIN	
Clutch	single dry-plate
Transmission	4-speed manual
Rear suspension	swing axle, coil springs
Rear axle ratio	4.44
Front suspension	independent
Frame	x-shaped oval tubular
GENERAL	
Wheelbase	3050 mm (120 in)
Track, front/rear	1480/1525 mm (58.2/60 in)
Brakes	drum
Steering ratio	17.9:1
Wheels	15 in steel disc
Tire size, front and rear	7.10x15 extra
Weight	1780 kg (3916 lb); convertible, 1830 kg (4026 lb)
Maximum speed	160 km/h (99.5 mph)
Acceleration	18 sec 0-100 km
Fuel consumption	16.5 ltr/100 km (14.2 mpg)
Gas tank capacity	72 ltr (19 gal)

300 trunk space with factory-fitted luggage options of this type are very satisfying for the owner, and enhance resale value considerably. (Mercedes-Benz)

The 300 sedan—grandness at a low price. Condition is foremost with this model due to its high cost of restoration and minimum restored value. (Mercedes-Benz)

61

TYPE: 300d	
ENGINE	
Type	6 cyl overhead camshaft (M 189)
Bore x stroke	85x88 mm (3.35x3.46 in)
Displacement	2996 cc (182.7 cu in)
Value operation	single overhead cam, chain driven
Compression ratio	8.55:1
Fuel system	Bosch injection pump
Horsepower	160 hp (DIN) @5300 rpm
Torque	24.2 mkg@4200 rpm (175 ft/lb)
CHASSIS & DRIVETRAIN	
Clutch	single dry-plate
Transmission	3-speed automatic
Rear suspension	single swing axle, coil springs
Rear axle ratio	4.67
Front suspension	independent front
Frame	x-shaped oval tubular
GENERAL	
Wheelbase	3150 mm (124 in)
Track, front/rear	1480/1525 mm (58.3/60.0 in)
Brakes	drum
Wheels	15 in steel disc
Tire size, front and rear	7.60x15 extra
Weight	1950 kg (4290 lb); automatic, 2000 kg (4400 lb)
Maximum speed	170 km/h (105.6 mph); automatic, 165 km/h (102.5 mph)
Acceleration	17 sec 0-100 km; automatic, 18 sec 0-100 km
Fuel consumption	17 ltr, super (13.7 mpg); automatic, 18 ltr, super (13 mpg)
Gas tank capacity	72 ltr (19 gal)

This is often a good gauge in determining the value of a collector car. From the high original cost of the 300 sedan, it does not follow that this car is relatively valuable today. It does follow that you get a very high level of elegant appointments, especially a very plush interior. If your desire to own an old Mercedes is based on an image of a grand touring car that will turn heads at every corner without emptying your bank account, a 300 sedan is worth strong consideration.

The 300 four-door convertible sedan, if it suits your fancy, is a very desirable collector piece. The car fits most of the requirements for desirability and, with room for five passengers, it is also a good car for the entire family. Mechanical and body parts, readily interchangeable with the sedan, are therefore quite plentiful.

The 300s were built on a tubular chassis very similar to that of the 220 and 170. Again, the threat of rust is a major concern. Considering the relatively modest resale value of the 300 sedan, it is important to purchase a car needing as little work as possible. It is easy to invest more in the restoration of a 300 than the completed car will be worth.

The 300c with automatic transmission was very stately in appearance.

The 300 engine, with its almost-square bore and stroke ratio was both efficient and smooth running. Its seven-main-bearing crank ensures high durability. The 300b engine had a higher compression ratio and slightly larger carburetors, adding 10 hp. The 300b also had larger brakes than the first 300s. Four-wheel independent suspension, featuring load control on the rear axle, made for an unusually pleasant ride.

The c modification involved a slight lowering (1½ inches) of the body and availability of an optional automatic transmission. The d variation had a slightly longer wheelbase (up from 3050 to 3150 mm, 119 to 123 in) and a higher compression ratio (up from 7.5:1 to 8.5:1). The most noticeable changes in the d model were the horsepower (160, up 35 from the b and c models), more window area and more modern rear fenders. The 300 convertibles offered the ultimate in open-air touring with plenty of room and luxurious appointments.

The very high cost of parts for all 300 models must be stressed. Few of these models were produced, and expensive tooling costs were spread out over a small number of cars. Parts can be shockingly expensive, so look for a car in the best condition.

300b cabriolet D, with rounded rear fenders common to 300 and 300c.

300d cabriolet D is distinguishable from the 300b and c by the more modern rear fender design, with a taillight similar to the 220SE cabriolet.

This 300c cabriolet D can be distinguished from the 300 and 300b by the vent space located just behind the driving lights. (Mercedes-Benz)

The 300d cabriolet D with the top down; a car for the collector with a large family. (Alex Dearborn)

In the 300S engine compartment, everything is easy to get at and quite simple in design. A bad point is the battery location. First, it is hard to get at and, second, battery acid can cause decay through to the footspace area of the interior.

300S and 300Sc, 1951-62

The 300S started production with just two cars in 1951 and 113 in 1952. This low-production automobile was aimed at the true sports and grand touring enthusiast with a financial position to match his or her tastes. Mercedes-Benz was successful at this type of marketing in the late 1920s and throughout the 1930s with the S, SS, SSK, 500K and 540K. The 300S had a 1953 price tag of about $12,500. That was close to ten times the price of a standard American family car, or the equivalent of three Cadillacs. The car was designed and built to be worth every penny of its high price, with the best leather, wood trim, large well-proportioned bodies and sophisticated mechanics for its time.

The 300S and 300Sc both used a tubular steel chassis frame. Restorers will appreciate

Facts for enthusiasts

The 300S chassis with solid oval tubular frame. The jacking points are clearly visible, one at each wheel (standard from 1933 to present).

The 300S never used unibody construction, but continued the solid chassis frame through 1963.

the structural strength of a solid chassis compared with unibody construction and the ease of working on the frame independent of the body. Both models also featured four-wheel independent suspension.

The carbureted 300S engine was very similar to the 300, 300b and 300c while the 300Sc engine, fitted with Bosch fuel injection, was basically similar to the 300d engine. The major difference between the Sc and SL engines was the engine mounts determined by the angle they were installed in the Sc or SL chassis. (The Sc engines stood upright while the SL engines were canted.) Capable of nearly 100 mph, the 300S and 300Sc offered the ultimate in comfortable and fast touring. Without question, the 300S and 300Sc fulfilled the basic requirements of greatness in a collectible car. Their beauty and mechanical sophistication has brought their value equal to that of the 300SL, with recent sales of the 300Sc being considerably higher than those of the gullwing coupe.

Both the 300S and 300Sc were offered in coupe, cabriolet A and roadster versions. The roadster is normally the most desirable primarily because of its disappearing top.

TYPE: 300S

ENGINE

Type	6-cyl overhead camshaft (M 188)
Bore x stroke	85x88 mm (3.35x3.46 in)
Displacement	2996 cc (182.7 cu in)
Valve operation	single overhead cam, chain driven
Compression ratio	7.8:1
Fuel system	3 downdraft carbs, Solex 40 PBJC
Horsepower	150 hp (DIN) @5000 rpm
Torque	23.5 mkg@3800 rpm (170 ft/lb)

CHASSIS & DRIVETRAIN

Clutch	single dry-plate
Transmission	4-speed manual
Rear suspension	swing axle, coil springs
Rear axle ratio	4.125
Front suspension	independent
Frame	x-shaped oval tubular

GENERAL

Wheelbase	2900 mm (114.2 in)
Track, front/rear	1480/1525 mm (58.2/60 in)
Brakes	drum
Steering ratio	21.4:1
Wheels	15 in steel disc
Tire size, front and rear	6.70x15 extra
Weight	1760 kg (3880 lb)
Maximum speed	176 km/h (109 mph)
Acceleration	15 sec 0-100 km
Fuel consumption	17 ltr, super/100 km (13.7 mpg)
Gas tank capacity	85 ltr (22 gal)

300S carbureted engine: You can see the radiator filler cap is under the hood rather than at the radiator mascot.

The 300SC dash was in veneer. The radio was standard and the speedometer read in kilometers. (Alex Dearborn)

TYPE: 300Sc

ENGINE

Type	6-cyl overhead camshaft (M 188)
Bore x stroke	85x88 mm (3.35x3.46 in)
Displacement	2996 cc (182.7 cu in)
Valve operation	single overhead cam, chain driven
Compression ratio	8.55:1
Fuel system	Bosch injection pump
Horsepower	175 hp (DIN) @5400 rpm
Torque	26 mkg@4300 rpm (188 ft/lb)

CHASSIS & DRIVETRAIN

Clutch	single dry-plate
Transmission	4-speed manual
Rear suspension	single pivot swing axle, coil springs
Rear axle ratio	4.44
Front suspension	independent
Frame	x-shaped oval tubular

GENERAL

Wheelbase	2900 mm (114.2 in)
Track, front/rear	1480/1525 mm (58.2/60 in)
Brakes	drum
Steering ratio	21.4:1
Wheels	15 in steel disc
Tire size, front and rear	6.70x15 extra
Weight	1780 kg (3924 lb)
Maximum speed	180 km/h (112 mph)
Acceleration	14 sec 0-100 km
Fuel consumption	17 ltr, super/100 km (13.7 mpg)
Gas tank capacity	85 ltr (22 gal)

The cabriolet A follows closely in desirability and, as in most cases, the coupe is in last position.

Different from the wooden-body-framed 170 and 220, the 300S and 300Sc used a metal body frame, saving the restorer considerable restoration headaches.

Replacement body accent chrome is in adequate supply, so it is not a large problem to the restorer. Many mechanical parts on the 300S and 300Sc are interchangeable with those of their less expensive relatives, the 300, 300b, 300c and 300d. Conversely, body parts are unique to these models and are extremely difficult to locate.

Production of the 300S (560 cars total) breaks down as follows: coupe, 216 cars; cabriolet, 203; and roadster, 141. Unlike the coupe and cabriolet which seat four, the roadster (with disappearing top) seats two, with a small rear space best suited to luggage.

The 300Sc was introduced in late 1955, and 200 cars were produced; ninety-eight coupes, forty-nine cabriolets and fifty-three roadsters.

This 300S cabriolet A was a test model, judging by the instrument mounted outside the windshield. The ski rack may have been a factory installation available to the public. (Mercedes-Benz)

The 300S and Sc roadster: The most desirable of the three body types, the roadster's disappearing top is beautiful, up or down. This is real luxury. All this machinery and beauty to propel two people down a winding road! The 300SC was the last two-seater grand road car offered by Mercedes-Benz. (Alex Dearborn)

300S coupe: Although the proportions may be deceiving, the 300S and SC are large cars with a definite feeling of luxury, with very large leather bucket seats, wood trim and a slightly detuned 300SL engine. The 300S and Sc offer elegance, comfort and speed, an important mix in any collectible car. (Alex Dearborn)

1956 300Sc roadster was distinguishable from the standard 300S by chrome edge trim on the fender wheel openings, wheel trim rings, and by the 300Sc fuel-injection system under the hood, plus opening side "quarter lights." See the Sc coupe photo.

The 300S and 300Sc have rapidly appreciated in value over the past several years, so there are few bargains to be found. The 300S and 300Sc mark DBAG's first attempt at a postwar luxury grand touring car. The styling is a successful adaptation of prewar classic lines, very unusual against the backdrop of the 1950s fins and futuristic features, but dictated by Daimler-Benz's postwar rebuilding process.

300SL gullwing, 1954-63

Before World War II, Mercedes-Benz was very successful in racing. In 1952, it dramatically reentered the racing scene with the introduction of an entirely new car—the 300SL sports racing car. This car featured a multitubular chassis and a highly tuned version of the 300 engine shared with the model 300 sedans. The 300SL became a regular production model in 1954. The two-passen-

Beautifully restored 300Sc coupe for contrast. (Tim Parker)

With its convertible top concealed and hardtop attached, this 300SL coupe-roadster is ready for long-distance touring in any weather. The unusual door handles pivot out when depressed with the thumb, using lever action to operate the door latch. (Mercedes-Benz)

The immortal gullwing (skis optional); one rare case of a coupe being more valuable than the roadster version. The side windows can be removed but not lowered, which can be a problem in warm weather. (Mercedes-Benz)

ger coupe, with its uniquely opening doors, became unofficially known as the 300SL gullwing.

A roadster at auction in Monterey, California, in August 1986. Note change of headlamp style. (Tim Parker)

In 1957, the 300SL roadster was introduced sporting a removable hardtop and a concealed soft top for all-weather usage.

Today, the 300SL is still Mercedes-Benz's most intriguing postwar sports car. Its racing-based six-cylinder, overhead cam, fuel-injected engine combined with powerful lines of the gullwing or roadster bodies offer collectors the rare combination of mechanical sophistication and styling elegance.

The 300SL gullwing coupe offered the sports car enthusiast a street car developed from a full-fledged racing car. The super-light designation, SL, described a revolutionary technique of using welded small-diameter steel tubing for the car's chassis and body frame. This technique, first developed in the aircraft industry, offered both structural strength and a great weight reduction.

Optional knock-offs, normally used for sports racing or rallying. Special options of this type always add to desirability. (Alex Dearborn)

The preproduction three-liter carbureted engine was soon modified with the addition of direct fuel injection, increased compression, a hotter camshaft and larger valves, which increased the 300's horsepower from 115 to the 300SL's 250 hp. In order to fit all this under a sleek, low hoodline, the engine was mounted at a forty-five-degree angle and used dry-sump lubrication.

The Bosch mechanical fuel-injection system used in the 300SL was the first of its kind to be used in a Mercedes gasoline-powered production car, and it set the trend for decades to follow. Although the 300SL was a new model, its owner benefited from Mercedes' prior racing experience which came from the racing version of the 300SL, the 300SLR.

The self-cooling finned brake drums of the 300SL, along with the vacuum servo-assisted master cylinder, was the most effective braking system yet offered by DBAG.

Depending upon gearing, a top speed of 150 mph was possible in fourth gear to 6000 rpm. This impressive statistic for 1954 points out the high level of mechanical sophistication of the 300SL gullwing.

The most obvious visual feature of the 300SL coupe was the upward-opening gull-wing doors. Mercedes considered these to be a compromise necessary for body strength, but the doors caught the eye of the public

---

TYPE: 300SL (gullwing)

ENGINE

Type	6-cyl overhead camshaft (M 198)
Bore x stroke	85x88 mm (3.35x3.46 in)
Displacement	2996 cc (182.7 cu in)
Valve operation	single overhead cam, chain driven
Compression ratio	8.55:1
Fuel system	Bosch injection pump
Horsepower	215 hp (DIN) @5800 rpm (240 hp SAE)
Torque	28mkg@4600 rpm (217 ft/lb@4800 rpm)

CHASSIS & DRIVETRAIN

Clutch	single dry-plate
Transmission	4-speed manual
Rear suspension	swing axle, coil springs
Rear axle ratio	3.64
Front suspension	independent
Frame	tubular space frame with light alloy body

GENERAL

Wheelbase	2400 mm (94.5 in)
Track, front/rear	1385/1435 mm (54.5/56.5 in)
Brakes	drum
Steering ratio	17.3:1
Wheels	15 in steel disc
Tire size, front and rear	6.50x15 super sport
Weight	1295 kg (2849 lb)
Maximum speed	3.64 axle, 235 km/h (145 mph)
Acceleration	8.7 sec 0-100 km/h
Fuel consumption	17 ltr, super/100 km (13.7 mpg)
Gas tank capacity	130 ltr (34 gal)

300SL trunk: The spare tire took up most of the trunk space leading to the much-desired option of fitted luggage behind the seats.

A very nice addition to any vintage Mercedes. This gullwing is fitted with two pieces of leather luggage. You can also see the original wool plaid seats. (Mercedes-Benz)

and continue to do so today. Normally, a coupe body is of less value to collectors than a roadster body, but the fascination of these doors creates an exception to this rule, making the two-passenger gullwing coupe more valuable than the 300SL roadster.

The coupe's interior is luxurious for such a high-performance sports car. The car was even available with two pieces of fitted luggage. Early versions used a wool plaid upholstery material, while later models were equipped with perforated leather. The dash was laid out nicely with a full array of instruments. The huge fuel tank left the car with a small trunk, with room only for a spare tire. The steering wheel tilted for easier access through the gullwing doors.

The windows in the gullwing doors were a pop-out style, making it necessary to stop the car for removal and installation. This, along with engine heat, could make for some rather uncomfortable summer driving. However, most owners feel that the car's performance and beauty more than compensate for this inconvenience.

300SL coupe-roadster, 1957-63

The 300SL roadster, introduced in 1957, continued the development of the 300SL coupe. The roadster preserved the basic lines of the gullwing without its steel roof and unique doors.

Mechanically, the roadster reached a higher level of technical development than did the coupe. In its final version in 1963, it was available with four-wheel disc brakes and an alloy engine block. Features such as these, as with all sophisticated mechanical improvements, can make a later car more valuable.

The roadster was also fitted with a unique and improved low-pivot rear swing axle. Rather than both axles pivoting from the differential, the left axle housing was fixed to the differential, allowing only the right axle to swing free of the differential. This design improved roadholding, especially in cornering.

When examining a 300SL coupe or roadster body, the biggest concern is rust. The eyebrows above the wheelhousings and the fenders themselves are very prone to trapping dirt and, consequently, to rust. The 300SL is very susceptible to rust around the headlights. It is a good idea to remove the headlights and check very carefully. Examine the grille area to see if it has been replaced, which is frequently done with poor results. The rocker panels, doors and hood, on the other hand, are aluminum and hence

This photo shows the leather interior of the 300SL gullwing; early models used wool plaid. (Alex Dearborn)

As you can see, the 300SL engine was mounted at a 45 degree angle to allow a low hoodline. The aluminum intake manifold used long air columns for more horsepower. (Alex Dearborn)

not as susceptible to corrosion—but check them over well.

Many 300SL engine parts are interchangeable with the less valuable 300b, 300c and 300d engines. In addition, thanks to the efforts of the Gull Wing Group, several mechanical components unique to the 300SL are now being manufactured again. (No one should own a 300SL without belonging to this club, which is a great place to find a car, parts, advice, restoration services and so on.) Take particular care in mechanical restoration and keep in mind that more demanding use will have been made of a mechanically sophisticated car.

The desirability of the 300SL makes it one Mercedes-Benz that definitely justifies the high cost of restoration. If you are looking for one of these cars, it pays to find a clean original or well-restored version rather than a project car. Modifications are difficult to bring back to original, and spare parts are hard to find and costly. It also pays to drive a 300SL to make sure it suits you. At low speeds the car will seem heavy, hard to steer

TYPE: 300SL (coupe-roadster)

ENGINE
Type . . . . 6-cyl overhead camshaft (M 198)
Bore x stroke . . . . 85x88 mm (3.35x3.46 in)
Displacement . . . . 2996 cc (182.7 cu in)
Valve operation . . . . single overhead cam,
 chain driven
Compression ratio 9.5:1
Fuel system . . . . Bosch injection pump
Horsepower . . . . 215 hp (DIN) @5800 rpm (240 hp SAE)
Torque . . . . 228 ft/lb

CHASSIS & DRIVETRAIN
Clutch . . . . single dry-plate
Transmission . . . . 4-speed manual
Rear suspension . . . . swing axle, coil springs
Rear axle ratio 3.64
Front suspension . . . . independent
Frame . . . . tubular space frame with light alloy body

GENERAL
Wheelbase . . . . 2400 mm (94.5 in)
Track, front/rear . . . . 1398/1448 mm (55.0/57.0 in)
Brakes . . . . drum
Steering ratio 17.3:1
Wheels . . . . 15 in steel disc
Tire size, front and rear . . . . 6.70x15 super sport
Weight . . . . 1330 kg (2926 lb)
Maximum speed . . . . 3.64 axle, 235 km/h (145 mph)
Acceleration . . . . 8.1 sec 0-100 km/h (US, 7.2 sec)
Fuel consumption . . . . 17 ltr, super/100 km (13.7 mpg)
Gas tank capacity . . . . 100 ltr (26 gal)

With mechanical sophistication and a beautiful body, the 300SL roadster is the epitome of its kind. The vent is for engine-space cooling, the rear cowl pad covers the convertible top storage area. The body is steel and the rocker panels, doors, trunk and hood lid are aluminum. The 300SL uses a single-jack mount for either side of the car. (Mercedes-Benz)

and almost awkward, but get it up over 70 mph and things change dramatically. The steering lightens and the entire car seems right at home. Remember that these cars have the rear swing-axle, a competent suspension in its day but less sophisticated than that of modern cars.

Among the most-sought-after options are the fitted luggage, a hardtop for the roadster and Rudge knock-off wheels for the coupe. The presence and condition of the belly pans is also something to check, although reproductions are now available, as is high-quality reproduction luggage.

During the six-year production run of the 300SL roadster, 1,858 cars were built. The majority still exist today.

300SE and 300SEL, 1961-67

The much-modernized 300 inherited the engine of the 300Sc and 300SL and the unibody of the 220SEb. The 300SE was designed for the same market as the 300S and 300Sc. It must have been Mercedes' opinion that the extravagant sports car buyer of the 1950s had become more practical. This is evidenced by the 300SE cabriolet offering a full rear seat, roomy trunk and air suspension. This is hardly the makings of a sports car, so the 300SE can probably be best described as a grand touring car.

The 300SE was offered in three bodies: two-door cabriolet, coupe and four-door sedan. This car will appeal to the collector looking for comfort, moderate performance and contemporary classic lines. Restorers will benefit, as the 300SE is a combination of previously existing models. Engine parts are available from the 300 sedan series, and chassis and body parts, from the less expensive 220SEb series.

The 300 engine was put into a fin-back sedan in 1961—a combination that was never very popular. In 1963, a longer-wheelbase 300SEL was also offered, and in 1965 both cars received new finless bodies. The 300 series was extended in 1962 to include a coupe and a two-door cabriolet with the

Definitely a modernized development of the 300SE cabriolet using the basic 300Sc engine with a 220SEb body with the addition of chrome molding over the wheelwells, sporty but now a four-seater. The SL is now the only remaining two-seater. (Mercedes-Benz)

same finless body styles as the smaller-engined 220Sb coupe and cabriolet.

The 300SEs were a great combination of luxury and performance, and today they can be good buys. Automatic and four-speed manual transmissions were available, along with the usual amenities such as air conditioning, power windows and a very effective air suspension system in both front and rear. Production of the 300SE coupe and cabriolet lasted until 1967. That year also marked the sixteenth consecutive production year for the 300 engine, and the 300SE undoubtedly benefited from much engineering development. In addition to trim differences, the post-1964 cars had 6x14 inch wheels while the early 300SEs had 5x13 inch wheels.

TYPE: 300SE/300SE (long)
300SE (coupe and convertible)

ENGINE
Type .... 6-cyl overhead camshaft (M 189)
Bore x stroke .... 85x88 mm (3.34x3.47 in)
Displacement .... 2996 cc (182.8 cu in)
Valve operation .... single overhead cam, chain driven
Compression ratio 8.7:1
Fuel system .... Bosch two-plunger pump
Horsepower .... 160 hp (DIN) @5000 rpm
Torque .... 25.6 mkg@3800 rpm

CHASSIS & DRIVETRAIN
Clutch .... single dry-plate
Transmission .... 4-speed manual and automatic
Rear suspension .... independent, coil springs, single-joint swing axle, air suspension
Rear axle ratio .... 3.92 or 3.75 automatic, 4.10
Front suspension .... independent
Frame .... unit frame and body

GENERAL
Wheelbase .... 2750 mm (108.3 in); SE long, 2850 mm (112.2 in)
Track, front/rear .... 1482/1490 mm (58.3/58.6 in)
Brakes .... disc
Steering ratio 17.3:1
Wheels .... 13 in steel disc
Tire size, front and rear 7.50x13
Weight .... 1580 kg (3476 lb); long, 1630 kg (3586 lb); coupe, 1600 kg (3520 lb); conv, 1700 kg (3740 lb)
Maximum speed .... 160 hp manual; 3.92 axle, 180 km/h (112 mph); automatic, 175 km/h
Acceleration .... 160 hp, 13 sec 0-100 km/h; 170 hp, 12 sec 0-100 km/h
Fuel consumption .... 17 ltr, super/100 km (13.7 mpg); automatic, 19 ltr (12.3 mpg)
Gas tank capacity .... 65 ltr (17.2 gal)

The same body as the 220SEb, 250SE and 280SE coupe was found on the 300SE coupe. It had the three-liter six-cylinder developed from the early 1950s 300.

more plentiful but tamer 450SEL in today's market.

```
TYPE: 300SEL 6.3
ENGINE
Type .................. V-8 overhead camshaft (M 100)
Bore x stroke ................ 103x95 mm (4.06x3.74 in)
Displacement ..................... 6332 cc (386.3 cu in)
Valve operation .................. single overhead cam,
   chain driven
Compression ratio ........................... 9.0:1
Fuel system ................ Bosch eight-plunger pump
Horsepower .................. 250 hp (DIN) @4000 rpm
Torque ................... 51 mkg@2800 rpm 369 ft/lb
CHASSIS & DRIVETRAIN
Clutch .......................... single dry-plate
Transmission ............ 4-speed manual and automatic
Rear suspension .. air springs, self leveling and air suspension,
   single-joint swing axle
Rear axle ratio ............................... 2.85
Front suspension ....................... independent
Frame ...................... unit frame and body
GENERAL
Wheelbase ...................... 2865 mm (112.8 in)
Track, front/rear ............. 1482/1490 mm (58.3/58.7 in)
Brakes .................................... disc
Steering ratio ........................... 15.7:1
Wheels ....................... 14 in steel disc
Tire size, front and rear .................. 205/70 VR 14
Weight ...................... 1740 kg (3828 lb)
Maximum speed .................. 220 km/h (137 mph)
Acceleration ..................... 6.5 sec 0-100 km/h
Fuel consumption ........ 15.5 ltr, super/100 km (15.2 mpg)
Gas tank capacity .................... 105 ltr (27.7 gal)
```

The 6.3 exhibited incredible roadholding characteristics for its day. Combine this with the 300 hp engine and you have what amounts to a "big, bad wolf in sheep's clothing." The car was capable of doing 0-60 mph in 6.5 seconds and had a top speed of 140 mph. Even though the 6.3 was described by *Road & Track* as "The greatest sedan in the world," it is still a sedan. Had it been offered as a convertible, it would surely be the most valuable Mercedes-Benz produced in the 1960s!

As with all later-model collector cars, it is wise to find a car in the best condition you can afford. Parts on the low-production 6.3 are available, but very expensive. Also remember that as the car becomes more sophisticated, maintenance becomes more difficult.

The complicated air ride system of the 6.3 can be a real headache and the transmission can develop harsh shifting problems. Otherwise, if carefully serviced, the 6.3s are trouble free. These cars are true thoroughbreds and demand special attention. At the time of printing, the 6.3 is one of the best bargains around, when considering potential future value.

Chapter 7

Sixties six-cylinder

The six-cylinder SEb series occupies an interesting middle ground in the range of collectible Mercedes-Benz cars. Models prior to the SEb are classics, but they come with certain problems which only a true enthusiast will see as part of the enjoyment of the hobby. Cars after the SEb were more modern and lacked the special feeling that comes from a link with the past as well as the handcrafted materials and quality work of low-production cars.

The 220SEb coupes and convertibles contained a very nice balance of old and new. Real leather, wool carpets and beautifully hand veneered wood trim were all standard. The 220SEb was a low-production model with fewer than 17,000 coupes and convertibles produced from 1960 to 1965. With this came a very dependable, easily maintained mechanical system with fuel injection, disc brakes, automatic transmission and a smooth ride.

220Sb and 220SEb, 1959-65

The 220Sb, introduced in 1959, was the last generation of the 220 series and was available only in a much-modernized fin-back four-door sedan. Although many feel the 220S lost something with its new finned

TYPE: 220Sb

ENGINE

Type	6-cyl overhead camshaft (M 127)
Bore x stroke	80x72.8 mm (3.16x2.87 in)
Displacement	2195 cc (133.9 cu in)
Valve operation	single overhead cam, chain driven
Compression ratio	8.7:1
Fuel system	2 Solex carbs
Horsepower	95 hp (DIN) @4800 rpm
Torque	18.4 mkg@3300 rpm

CHASSIS & DRIVETRAIN

Clutch	single dry-plate
Transmission	4-speed manual
Rear suspension	single-joint swing axle, coil springs
Rear axle ratio	4.10
Front suspension	independent
Frame	unit frame and body

GENERAL

Wheelbase	2750 mm (108.3 in)
Track, front/rear	1470/1485 mm (57.9/58.5 in)
Brakes	drum
Steering ratio	21.4:1
Wheels	13 in steel disc
Tire size, front and rear	6.70x13 sport
Weight	1380 kg (3036 lb)
Maximum speed	172 km/h (107 mph)
Acceleration	14 sec 0-100 km/h
Fuel consumption	14 ltr, super/100 km (16.75 mpg)
Gas tank capacity	65 ltr (17.2 gal)

★★★★	**220SEb cabriolet, 250SE cabriolet, 280SE cabriolet, 230SL, 250SL and 280SL**
★★★	**220SEb coupe, 250SE coupe and 280SE coupe**
★	**250C, 250CE and 220Sb**

body design, it was an extremely dependable family car. Its brother, the 220SEb, was also available in the normal sedan, but drew the most attention with the coupe and convertible models. These bodies remained largely

220SEb convertible is not as rare as its predecessors. With replaceable parts more accessible, the restoration of the SEb is less difficult than for earlier models. (Alex Dearborn)

unchanged until 1972. The body designs proved to be more timeless than the mechanical design and were used to body the 250SE, 280SE and 300SE. These were abandoned only with the introduction of the modern S-class body styles in the early 1970s.

One interesting change in the 220SEb two-door was the substantial increase in rear seat room compared with that of the 220SE of the 1950s.

The coupe and convertible versions are worth far more than the sedans, and the convertible is worth more than the coupe.

In its final stage of development in 1965, the mechanical sophistication of the 220SEb had increased dramatically from its beginning in the 1951 model 220. These advances included fuel injection, disc brakes, an increase in horsepower from eighty to 134, a much improved suspension system and a heater that actually worked!

When inspecting a 220Sb or 220SEb, remember that these cars used a unibody construction and therefore are very vulnerable to some serious rust problems. The bumpers

220Sb and 220SEb continued modernization can be seen in the straight body lines, less noticeable hood and fender separation, con-toured bumpers and double headlights. Also, the larger rear seat steals some of the sportiness of its predecessors. (Alex Dearborn)

have always been very susceptible to dents and rust. However, they are less troublesome in terms of chrome molding than their 220 and 220SE predecessors. Pay special attention to models with automatic transmissions; in particular, look for erratic and harsh shifting.

The 220SEb coupe and convertible are excellent choices for those looking for easy maintenance, dependability, civilized touring and a touch of classic style with moderate performance.

Late six-cylinder, 1965-72

Developing proven success, the 220S six-cylinder 2.2 liter engine was bored out to 2.3, 2.5 and 2.8 liters, respectively, for the 230, 250 and 280 S and SE models. This expansion exemplified Mercedes' adaptation to the public's demand for a wide range of models.

The model 230 used the fin-style body of the older 190 and 220 gas and diesel models. The 250 and 280 (S and SE) coupes and convertibles used the same body as the 220SEb coupe and convertible. However, a new

TYPE: 220SEb (sedan, coupe and convertible)

ENGINE
Type .... 6-cyl overhead camshaft (M 127)
Bore x stroke .... 80x72.8 mm (3.16x2.87 in)
Displacement .... 2195 cc (113.9 cu in)
Valve operation .... single overhead cam, chain driven
Compression ratio 8.7:1
Fuel system .... Bosch two-plunger pump
Horsepower .... 120 hp (DIN) @4800 rpm
Torque .... 19.3 mkg@3900 rpm

CHASSIS & DRIVETRAIN
Clutch .... single dry-plate
Transmission .... 4-speed manual and automatic
Rear suspension .... single-joint swing axle, coil springs
Rear axle ratio 4.10
Front suspension .... independent
Frame .... unit frame and body

GENERAL
Wheelbase .... 2750 mm (108.3 in)
Track, front/rear .... 1482/1485 mm (58.3/58.4 in)
Brakes .... disc, front; drum, rear
Steering ratio 22.7:1
Wheels .... 13 in steel disc
Tire size, front and rear .. coupe, 7.25x13; convertible, 7.50x13
Weight ..... coupe, 1410 kg (3102 lb); conv, 1510 kg (3322 lb)
Maximum speed .... 172 km/h (107 mph)
Acceleration .... 14 sec 0-100 km/h
Fuel consumption .... 14 ltr, super/100 km (16.75 mpg); automatic, 15 ltr (15.6 mpg)
Gas tank capacity .... 65 ltr (17.2 gal)

This very successful body of the 220SEb coupe and convertible referred to as the "highline" body ranged in production from 1959 with the 220SEb through 1972 with the 300SEb. (Alex Dearborn)

four-door body, developed from the 220SEb convertible styling, was introduced with the 250SE sedan. Referred to as the highline body style, it became one of Mercedes most popular designs and carried through the 250SE, 280S and 280SE, 3.5, 300SE, 300SEL, 3.5, 4.5 and 6.3, until 1972.

```
TYPE: 250SE (coupe and convertible)
ENGINE
Type .................. 6-cyl overhead camshaft (M 129)
Bore x stroke ................. 82x78.8 mm (3.23x3.1 in)
Displacement ..................... 2496 cc (152.3 cu in)
Valve operation ................... single overhead cam,
  chain driven
Compression ratio .......................... 9.3:1
Fuel system ................... Bosch six-plunger pump
Horsepower .................. 150 hp (DIN) @5500 rpm
Torque ...................... 22 mkg@4200 rpm
CHASSIS & DRIVETRAIN
Clutch .......................... single dry-plate
Transmission ............. 4-speed manual and automatic
Rear suspension ............... independent, coil springs,
  single-joint swing axle
Rear axle ratio .......................... 3.92
Front suspension ................... independent front
Frame ...................... unit frame and body
GENERAL
Wheelbase ...................... 2750 mm (108.3 in)
Track, front/rear ....... 1482/1485 mm (58.3/58.5 in)
Brakes .................................... disc
Steering ratio ........................... 22.7:1
Wheels ........................ 14 in steel disc
Tire size, front and rear ......... 7.35 H 14 or 185 H 14
Weight ........ 1510 kg (3322 lb); coupe, 1490 kg (3278 lb);
  conv, 1575 kg (3465 lb)
Maximum speed .................. 193 km/h (120 mph);
  automatic, 188 km/h (117 mph)
Acceleration ................. 12 sec 0-100 km/h;
  automatic, 13 sec 0-100 km/h
Fuel consumption ......... 16 ltr, super/100 km (14.7 mpg);
  automatic, 17 ltr, super (13.7 mpg)
Gas tank capacity ................... 82 ltr (21.7 gal)
```

Standard 220Sb sedan: Although dated, this body style has aged fairly gracefully. The fins were, no doubt, a result of American influence. (Mercedes-Benz)

The 250SE and 280SE coupes and convertibles are the best choices for those who want the most style, dependability and appreciation potential for the most reasonable investment.

Although parts are readily available for these models, it is normally more economical to purchase a car in the best possible condition. As with their predecessors, the 220, the 250 and the 280 use unibody construction, making rust a very important consideration. These are truly classic cars yet very dependable for hobby or even daily use. The rear seat of the coupes and convertible 250 and 280 S and SE have much more room than the 220S and 220SE of the fifties.

250SE and 280SE, 1965-72

The 250SE and 280SE were offered as a sedan or very elegant coupe or convertible. The 250S and 280S, however, were available only as sedans.

Modifications from the 220SEb were a larger bore and stroke, adding 300 cc to the 250SE and the 280SE. Tire diameter was increased from thirteen inches to fourteen inches. A horizontal-mount hydropneumatic (oil-air) compensating shock absorber was mounted above the rear axle to control ride height and provide a more smooth and stable ride. Four-wheel disc brakes were also added.

The interior remained finely crafted with leather, wood trim and wool carpets. Chrome appointments also remained the same. Although the wheelbase did not change through the full series, the 280SE body was shortened by three inches.

Frequently, additional mechanical sophistication will lead to a greater chance of failure. This is merely because the more things that there are to go wrong, the greater the probability that one will go wrong. However, this is not the case with the Mercedes fuel-injection system, even though it is more complex than standard carburetion. Bosch started researching fuel injection in the twenties and Mercedes began to use it in 1936 with the 260 diesel. Gasoline injection began with the 300SL in 1952. By the time of the 250SE, fuel injection had become extremely dependable, vulnerable only to extremely high mileage, dirty fuel and the most common villain, the human tinkerer.

230SL, 250SL and 280SL, 1963-71

The 230SL, 250SL and 280SL continued the superlight development where the 190SL left off. These three versions can be looked at as one series with progressively larger engines—2.3, 2.5 and 2.8 liters, respectively. The 250SL and 280SL engines were basically the same as their counterparts in the 250SE and 280SE sedans. Although this series, which ran from 1963-71, underwent almost no changes in body style, it continually received updates in the mechanics. The major changes were as follows: The 230 and 250 maintained the same compression ratio of 9.3:1, with the 280 being increased to 9.5:1. Horsepower outputs were 150 in the 230SL, 160 in the 250SL and 180 in the 280SL. The 230SL was fitted with front disc brakes while the 250SL and 280SL went to four-wheel disc brakes. All versions used vacuum servo-assist brake systems, with the 280SL using a slightly larger unit.

All three models were available with a four- or five-speed manual gearbox (both of which are quite rare), or a four-speed automatic. The rear axle was again the single-pivot independent suspension type, developed from the 300SL roadster.

The 230SL engine was a direct development from the 220SE fuel-injected model and offered a considerable increase in horsepower over the 190SL.

When the 230SL was introduced in 1963, its styling made it a hallmark among grand touring cars. Even today, the crisp lines and pagoda roof still look fresh.

In terms of performance and its market, the 230SL sat squarely between its predecessors, the 190SL and the 300SL. It was a much more usable car in every way, and because it was so competent with no real quirks to its character, it was perceived as a much less interesting car by enthusiasts. The truth is that the 230, 250 and 280SLs

Continuing the line of removable hardtops, the 230SL is considered by many sports car purists to be the best of the post-300SL "SL" series. Their feelings are based on the fact that later SLs became too civilized, with softer suspension, air-pollution equipment, more weight and so on. (Mercedes-Benz)

The 250SL was a short-lived version, being produced for one year until the production of the 280SL. Its rarity does not really affect its value, since it is basically the same as the 230SL. (Mercedes-Benz)

TYPE: 230SL	
ENGINE	
Type	6-cyl overhead camshaft (M 127)
Bore x stroke	82x72.8 mm (3.23x2.87 in)
Displacement	2306 cc (140.7 cu in)
Valve operation	single overhead cam, chain driven
Compression ratio	9.3:1
Fuel system	Bosch six-plunger pump
Horsepower	150 hp (DIN) @5500 rpm
Torque	20 mkg@4200 rpm
CHASSIS & DRIVETRAIN	
Clutch	single dry-plate
Transmission	4-speed manual and automatic
Rear suspension	single-joint swing axle, coil springs
Rear axle ratio	3.75
Front suspension	independent
Frame	unit frame and body
GENERAL	
Wheelbase	2400 mm (94.5 in)
Track, front/rear	1486/1487 mm (58.5/58.5 in)
Brakes	disc front; drum rear
Steering ratio	22.7:1
Wheels	14 in steel disc
Tire size, front and rear	185 HR 14 radial
Weight	roadster, 1300 kg (2860 lb); coupe, 1380 kg (3036 lb)
Maximum speed	200 km/h (124 mph); automatic, 195 km/h (121 mph)
Acceleration	11 sec 0-100 km/h; automatic, 13 sec 0-100 km/h
Fuel consumption	14 ltr, super/100 km (16.75 mpg)
Gas tank capacity	65 ltr (17.2 gal)

250SL insignia was a means of designation used since World War II; chrome insignia was attached to the trunk lid. (Tim Parker)

handle much better than the 300SL. They are much more powerful than the 190SL, and are more comfortable, easier to maintain and safer than either.

These SLs were sold as coupes (removable hardtop only), convertibles (soft top only) and coupe/convertibles (both tops) at the option of the buyer. The soft top disappeared beneath an aluminum cover. The bucket seats were very large and there was ample luggage space behind the seats and in the spacious trunk. Options included leather interior, power steering, whitewall tires, radio, fitted luggage and a transverse rear seat, most often found in coupe models.

As said earlier, the main differences within this series were mechanical, and the distinctions were many. The 230SL had disc brakes at the front only; when the 250SL arrived in 1967, it had four-wheel disc brakes, a larger fuel tank and engine changes including seven main bearings instead of four and provision for an oil cooler. Torque was increased but there was no noticeable increase in performance. The 280SL, introduced in 1968, had a redesigned engine, as it was the first model with emission controls. Again, performance improvement was limited to slightly better acceleration. The interior trim of the 280SL was also more luxurious than that of the earlier models. Power steering became available as an option in late 1970.

Many other minor changes were made, but all other things being equal, the 1970-71 280SL, the last year of production, is probably the most desirable. Its refined design, coupled with the higher-torque engine, give it a clear advantage.

While the 230, 250 and 280SLs were the last Mercedes-Benz sports cars to use the venerable rear swing-axle, they were the first Mercedes-Benz sports cars available with air conditioning and automatic transmissions. The standard transmission was the four-speed manual gearbox with wide ratios, but a few 280SLs built after May 1969 had an optional five-speed ZF gearbox, a very rare and desirable feature today. Most cars, especially later models, have four-speed automatics.

During spirited driving, these SLs' biggest weakness surfaces—the rear suspension. The design allows radical camber changes to take place, especially under heavy braking. When braking hard into a corner, the rear end rises, causing excessive positive rear camber and a loss of traction. The driver then eases off the brakes and traction is regained; however, if the brakes are reapplied, the cycle starts again. The change in rear camber is obviously a problem in hard corners, where imprudent application or release of the throttle can lead to spectacular results.

When inspecting one of these models, check the engine numbers very carefully, as the mechanically fuel injected 230, 250 and 280SL engines are easily interchanged. Also inspect the engine head because it, like other Mercedes engines, can be corroded by incorrect coolant. If possible, run a leakdown test of the coolant system before you decide to buy. Timing chain wear is not unusual and is easy to rectify. Again, as in many Mercedes-Benz models, the exhaust systems are relatively short-lived.

These SLs share three common enemies: rust, brakes and exhaust. When looking for

---

TYPE: 250SL

ENGINE

Type	6-cyl overhead camshaft (M 129)
Bore x stroke	82x78.8 mm (3.23x3.1 in)
Displacement	2496 cc (152.3 cu in)
Valve operation	single overhead cam, chain driven
Compression ratio	9.3:1
Fuel system	Bosch six-plunger pump
Horsepower	150 hp (DIN) @5500 rpm
Torque	22 mkg@4200 rpm

CHASSIS & DRIVETRAIN

Clutch	single dry-plate
Transmission	4-speed manual and automatic
Rear suspension	independent, coil springs, single-joint swing axle
Rear axle ratio	3.69
Front suspension	independent
Frame	unit frame and body

GENERAL

Wheelbase	2400 mm (94.5 in)
Track, front/rear	1486/1487 mm (58.5/58.5 in)
Brakes	disc
Steering ratio	22.7:1
Wheels	14 in steel disc
Tire size, front and rear	185 H 14 radial
Weight	roadster, 1300 kg (2860 lb); coupe, 1380 kg (3036 lb)
Maximum speed	200 km/h (124 mph); automatic, 195 km/h (121 mph)
Acceleration	11 sec 0-100 km/h; automatic, 13 sec 0-100 km/h
Fuel consumption	14 ltr, super/100 km (16.75 mpg)
Gas tank capacity	82 ltr (21.7 gal)

A 1971 280SL with all the latest developments in place. As a road car it is superlight, fast and very comfortable. American versions were slightly hampered by air-pollution equipment. (Alex Dearborn)

rust, thoroughly examine the front fenders and rocker panels, especially around the

```
┌─────────────────────────────────────────────┐
│ TYPE: 280SL                                   │
│ ENGINE                                        │
│ Type ................. 6-cyl overhead camshaft (M 130) │
│ Bore x stroke .............. 86.5x78.8 mm (3.41x3.10 in) │
│ Displacement ................... 2778 cc (169.5 cu in) │
│ Valve operation ................. single overhead cam, │
│   chain driven                                │
│ Compression ratio ......................... 9.5:1 │
│ Fuel system .................. Bosch six-plunger pump │
│ Horsepower ................. 170 hp (DIN) @5700 rpm │
│ Torque ....................... 24.5 mkg@4250 rpm │
│ CHASSIS & DRIVETRAIN                           │
│ Clutch ....................... single dry-plate │
│ Transmission ............ 4-speed manual and automatic │
│ Rear suspension ............... independent, coil springs, │
│   single-joint swing axle                     │
│ Rear axle ratio ............................. 4.08 │
│ Front suspension ...................... independent │
│ Frame ...................... unit frame and body │
│ GENERAL                                       │
│ Wheelbase ...................... 2400 mm (94.5 in) │
│ Track, front/rear ............ 1486/1487 mm (58.5/58.5 in) │
│ Brakes ........................................ disc │
│ Steering ratio .......................... 17.2:1 │
│ Wheels ......................... 14 in steel disc │
│ Tire size, front and rear ................ 185 H 14 radial │
│ Weight ...................... roadster, 1340 kg (2948 lb); │
│   coupe, 1420 kg (3124 lb)                    │
│ Maximum speed .................. 195 km/h (121 mph); │
│   automatic, 190 km/h (118 mph)               │
│ Acceleration ...................... 10 sec 0-100 km/h; │
│   automatic, 11 sec 0-100 km/h                │
│ Fuel consumption ........ 14 ltr, super/100 km (16.75 mpg) │
│ Gas tank capacity ................... 82 ltr (21.7 gal) │
└─────────────────────────────────────────────┘
```

This Pininfarina-bodied 230SL was ordered by Axel Springer as a one-off custom. (Mercedes-Benz)

headlights, behind the front wheels and under the doors. Also carefully check the inner fender panels and all four fender lips. One advantage to this series is the factory accessibility and low price of body parts. However, chrome parts are scarce—pay close attention to the condition of the grille and bumpers, as they are very expensive to replace.

As you inspect the undercarriage, check the front cross-member, the floor pan on the driver's side and the trunk floor. Since the doors, trunk lid and engine lid (along with the tonneau cover) are made of aluminum, they do not rust, but they are susceptible to dents.

If the car you are considering is missing the hardtop or soft top, remember that these are expensive.

Deciding between a 230SL and a 280SL is difficult. The 230SL, because of its suspension design, had a very firm and sporty feel on the road. The 280SL had a softer, more cushioned ride that lacked the "road feel" that was so prevalent with the 230SL.

Although the 280SL had the highest horsepower output, there was little difference in performance because of the growing use of pollution control equipment. The 280SL was the result of engineering evolution, but it is arguable whether this engineering was a benefit or a detriment. These differences can best be summed up this way: If you are looking for the maximum in true sports car feel, then the 230SL is for you; if you are looking for comfort and the greatest mechanical development, then look to the 280SL. Generally, the 250SL falls in the same category as the 230SL.

Slightly fewer than 50,000 of these sporty, high-performance cars were produced, so they are relatively easy to locate. The 230, 250 and 280SL series has been steadily growing in popularity among collectors, and this trend will likely continue, making these cars a good investment.

Chapter 8

Early V-8

600, 1963-81

In 1963, Mercedes introduced the model 600, the world's most luxurious limousine, to replace the model 300. The 600 was a completely new design and incorporated the latest mechanical advances of the day with the grand luxury of a full-size limousine body. The car was beyond criticism and a total sensation. Even today, the model 600 is considered to be one of the finest luxury limousines.

The 6.3 liter, 300 hp engine was DBAG's first production V-type eight-cylinder engine. The fuel-injected, overhead cam V-8 was powerful enough to propel the 5,000 pound, short-wheelbase model 600 to nearly 130 mph. Even the 6,200 pound long-wheelbase Pullman model could achieve 124 mph. This figure decreased in versions modified for chiefs of state, who required armor plating.

The 600 was offered in three production styles: the 600 four-door limousine, the 600 Pullman six-door limousine and the 600 Pullman landaulette (a six-door with a convertible top over the passenger area). There were numerous special variations of these models, since bodywork and equipment could be tailored to the individual customer.

Production began with just three cars produced late in 1963, the first year, but it rose to nearly 400 cars per year in the late sixties. By 1973, production had slowed to

Sedate lines at the rear of the 600 sport twin tail exhausts and rear window drapes. (Tim Parker)

★★★★★   **280SE 3.5 cabriolet, and 600 landaulette**
★★★★   **600**
★★★   **280SE 3.5 coupe, 280SE 3.5 sedan, 280SE 4.5 sedan and 300SEL 6.3**

under 100 cars per year, making the later models more rare. When production ended in 1981, a total of 2,677 model 600s had been built. This broke down into 2,190 standard 600s, 428 600 Pullmans and fifty-nine landaulettes. The landaulette is the rarest and most desirable production version, but at least one of the two specially built two-door coupes is known to survive.

The 600 offered the ultimate in mechanical sophistication and luxury with such features as air suspension, adjustable shock absorbers, central locking system, hydraulic trunk operation, adjustable steering wheel, two separate heating and air conditioning systems, rear seat bar and refrigerator, flower vase and vanity—all for roughly $25,000.

Suspension in the 600 was unique, with heavy rubber airbags added to the four-wheel independent system. These bags were used to raise and lower the car and gave the passenger a true feeling of riding on air. The suspension system was complicated, with multiple valves and controls, all run at the fingertips of the driver. With these dimensions, the car was offered only with an automatic transmission.

The transmission and air suspension are the most common problems with the model 600. The complicated height-adjustment system also causes troubles. On the other hand, the engine, just as in the 6.3, is extremely durable.

As with all mechanical systems, the greater the complexity, the greater the possibility for failure, which leads to the greater cost of maintenance. Parts are extremely expensive and often difficult to install. With this in mind, anyone interested in the model 600

The short-wheelbase 600 limousine with its unmistakable presence. Its sophistication is much more than skin deep with 6.3 liter fuel-injected engine, air suspension, hydraulically operated doors and trunk, and almost any interior option imaginable. (Mercedes-Benz)

A rare 600 two-door coupe—one of two built in 1964. Generally, if you want a 600, normally you want a chauffeur and plenty of leg room.

Perfect race car tender—600 landaulette. Note change of headlamp style. (Tim Parker)

The 600 landaulette is perfect for either sporty dignitary or Pope. (Mercedes-Benz)

should look long and hard for one in excellent mechanical condition.

A total of 2,677 model 600s were produced, making the car quite rare and an excellent investment. Keep in mind that ultimate prestige and luxury have their price

600 interior might include television, stereo and cocktails. (Tim Parker)

TYPE: 600	
ENGINE	
Type	V-8 overhead camshaft (M 100)
Bore x stroke, mm/inches	103x95 mm
(4.06x3.74 in)	
Displacement	6332 cc (386.3 cu in)
Valve operation	single overhead cam, chain driven
Compression ratio	9.0:1
Fuel system	Bosch eight-plunger pump
Horsepower	250 hp (DIN) @ 4000 rpm
Torque	51 mkg@2800 rpm 369 ft/lb
CHASSIS & DRIVETRAIN	
Clutch	Single dry-plate
Transmission	4-speed automatic
Rear suspension	air springs, self leveling and air suspension, single-joint swing axle
Rear axle ratio	3.23
Front suspension	independent front
Frame	unit frame and body
GENERAL	
Wheelbase	3200 mm (126 in)
Track, front/rear	1587/1581 (62.5/62 in)
Brakes	disc
Steering ratio	17.3:1
Wheels	15 in steel disc
Tire size, front and rear	9.00x15
Weight	2470 kg (5434 lb)
Maximum speed	205 km/h (127 mph)
Acceleration	10 sec 0-100 km/h
Fuel consumption	24 ltr, super/100 km (15.2 mpg)
Gas tank capacity	112 ltr (27.7 gal)

Mercedes-Benz Typ 600
Pullman-Limousine 6 Türen
1964 – 1981

The six-passenger Pullman limousine came with four or six doors. Normally the rear seats faced each other. (Mercedes-Benz)

and, therefore, a model 600 will command top dollar. A clean, well-maintained original car can easily cost twice as much as one needing restoration.

300SEL 6.3 liter, 1968-72

Developed as a sportier version of the model 600, the 1968 300SEL 6.3 used the same fuel-injected engine as the grand 600. In addition, the 6.3 borrowed the hydraulic air suspension system of its bigger brother. This car lacked very little in the way of mechanical sophistication and was billed as "The fastest sedan in the world." The 6.3 was only offered in the four-door 300SEL sedan body, forcing it to compete with the more plentiful but tamer 450SEL in today's market.

The 6.3 exhibited incredible roadholding characteristics for its day. Combine this with the 300 hp engine and you have what amounts to a "big, bad wolf in sheep's clothing." The car was capable of doing 0-60 mph in 6.5 seconds and had a top speed of 140

Musclebound in the extreme. Developed from the 6.3 liter engine of the 1964 600, the 300SEL 6.3 had an additional 45 hp. (*Road & Track*)

The 6.3 was claimed to be the fastest four-door production car in the world, though you wouldn't recognize this wolf in sheep's clothing. The 6.3 liter engine propelled this 5,000 pound car 0-60 in less than eight seconds. Notice the jack mounts located just behind the front wheel and just ahead of the rear wheels. A good telltale test for rust on unibody Mercedes is to jack the car up at all four jack mounts. If there is serious deterioration of the unibody construction, it may show in weakness at these points. (*Road & Track*)

mph. Even though the 6.3 was described by *Road & Track* as "The greatest sedan in the world," it is still a sedan. Had it been offered as a convertible, it would surely be the most valuable Mercedes-Benz produced in the 1960s!

As with all later-model collector cars, it is wise to find a car in the best condition you can afford. Parts on the low-production 6.3 are available, but very expensive. Also remember that as the car becomes more sophisticated, maintenance becomes more difficult.

The complicated air ride system of the 6.3 can be a real headache and the transmission can develop harsh shifting problems. Otherwise, if carefully serviced, the 6.3s are trouble free. Watch the rear axle; it's unique to the 6.3 and will break with excessive use of the available power. These cars are true thoroughbreds and demand special attention. At the time of printing, the 6.3 is one of the best bargains around, when considering potential future value.

US-specification 280SE 3.5 cabriolet with side-marker lights on the rear fenders and changed rear license plate lights. (Tim Parker)

TYPE: 300SEL 6.3

ENGINE

Type	V-8 overhead camshaft (M 100)
Bore x stroke	103x95 mm (4.06x3.74 in)
Displacement	6332 cc (386.3 cu in)
Valve operation	single overhead cam, chain driven
Compression ratio	9.0:1
Fuel system	Bosch eight-plunger pump
Horsepower	250 hp (DIN) @4000 rpm
Torque	51 mkg@2800 rpm 369 ft/lb

CHASSIS & DRIVETRAIN

Clutch	single dry-plate
Transmission	4-speed manual and automatic
Rear suspension	air springs, self leveling and air suspension, single-joint swing axle
Rear axle ratio	2.85
Front suspension	independent
Frame	unit frame and body

GENERAL

Wheelbase	2865 mm (112.8 in)
Track, front/rear	1482/1490 mm (58.3/58.7 in)
Brakes	disc
Steering ratio	15.7:1
Wheels	14 in steel disc
Tire size, front and rear	205/70 VR 14
Weight	1740 kg (3828 lb)
Maximum speed	220 km/h (137 mph)
Acceleration	6.5 sec 0-100 km/h
Fuel consumption	15.5 ltr, super/100 km (15.2 mpg)
Gas tank capacity	105 ltr (27.7 gal)

The 1971 280SE 3.5 cabriolet with basically the same body as the 1961 220SE cabriolet. European version shown here.

With its 280SE body and powerful V-8 engine, the 3.5 is another example of mechanical sophistication and beautiful body lines harmoniously blended. (This type of designation on the trunk lid indicates the body type on the left and engine displacement on the right.) As should be expected, it is one of the most-sought-after of all Mercedes. (Mercedes-Benz)

The 3.5 coupe is very elegant but less expensive than the convertible. It is also less costly to restore than the convertible because the interior does not generally suffer as much from exposure to the weather. (Mercedes-Benz)

From the rear, showing correct badging and chrome work. (Tim Parker)

280SE 3.5: another masterpiece of wood veneering. The tach hints that this is not just a comfortable road car. A skilled driver could make you wonder where the beauty stops and the beast begins. (Alex Dearborn)

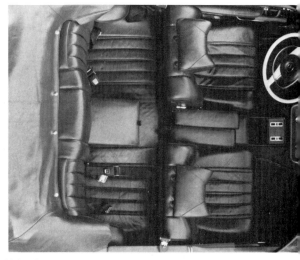

With fold-down rear armrest and contoured rear seat, 280SE 3.5 seating is best described as 2+2 Mercedes. Most German cars use thicker, surface-died leather, which shows scratches and cracks, but holds its shape better than English-type vat-died leathers. (Alex Dearborn)

280SE 3.5, 1969-71

The 280SE 3.5 coupe and convertible were Mercedes' first V-8-powered sports cars. The combination of superb performance and elegant styling makes the 3.5 a very desirable car. The 3.5 also offered something the 6.3 did not: a convertible.

This new 280SE used the same basic body as the 280SE six-cylinder. The new interior featured more wood, and leather upholstery was standard. This was a low-production car for its day, with just 4,502 units produced, most of them cabriolets.

The 3.5 V-8 introduced the Engine of Tomorrow for Mercedes. This highly advanced engine with its electronic fuel injection and transistorized ignition later developed into the engine for the 350 and 450 S-class series of the seventies. This development marked the end of an era and a new direction in automotive engineering.

The move from mechanical to electronic fuel injection is not always appreciated by auto enthusiasts and collectors, as most find the mechanical systems more interesting. Regardless, the 280SE 3.5 is one of the most desirable Mercedes-Benzes.

TYPE: 280SE 3.5 (coupe and convertible)	
ENGINE	
Type	V-8 overhead camshaft (M 116)
Bore x stroke	92x65.8 mm (3.62x2.59 in)
Displacement	3499 cc (213.5 cu in)
Valve operation	single overhead cam, chain driven
Compression ratio	9.5:1
Fuel system	Bosch electronic
Horsepower	200 hp (DIN) @5800 rpm
Torque	29.2 mkg@4000 rpm
CHASSIS & DRIVETRAIN	
Clutch	single dry-plate
Transmission	4-speed manual and automatic
Rear suspension	independent, coil springs, single-joint swing axle
Rear axle ratio	3.69
Front suspension	independent
Frame	unit frame and body
GENERAL	
Wheelbase	2750 mm (108.3 in)
Track, front/rear	1482/1485 mm (58.4/58.6 in)
Brakes	disc
Steering ratio	17.3:1
Wheels	14 in steel disc
Tire size, front and rear	7.35 H 14 or 185 H 14
Weight	convertible, 1574 kg (3463 lb); coupe, 1655 kg (3641 lb)
Maximum speed	205 km/h (127 mph)
Acceleration	9.5 sec 0-100 km/h
Fuel consumption	13 ltr, super/100 km (18 mpg)
Gas tank capacity	82 ltr (21.7 gal)

Not a coupe nor a cabriolet but nevertheless a neat sedan—280SE 4.5 is worth something in the investment game, especially in this condition. (Tim Parker)

Chapter 9

Modern V-8

350SL and 450SL, 1970-80

During the late 1960s it became very apparent that the stiffening government safety and emissions regulations would require a new model to replace the ten-year-old 230, 250 and 280SL series. The new body design would have to be larger and heavier and, therefore, would require a larger engine to compensate. The resulting car became one of the world's best grand touring cars.

In 1970, the 350SL replaced the 280SL as Mercedes-Benz's luxury sports car and became the firsts SL to use the V-8 engine. The 350SL used the 3.5 liter engine of the 280SE 3.5 and an all-new two-seater roadster body with removable hardtop. The body styling of the 350SL established the basic body lines Mercedes used for the next ten years.

The 1971 US model of the 350SL used the fuel-injected 4.5 liter engine. This made the 350 and 450 basically the same car. Eventually, in 1972, the 4.5 got its own identity in the 450SL. The 1974 and later 450SL also had the less-than-attractive US safety bumpers. As emission and crash-test require-

ments stiffened, the 450SL marked the beginning of more serious differences between US and European models.

The 450SL was equipped with the 4.5 liter overhead cam engine. The increase in displacement and additional emission controls produced excessive heat in the engine bay, making vapor lock a common ailment. In 1978, DBAG added a device that used air conditioner Freon to keep the gasoline cool. This can be retrofitted to earlier 350 and 450SLs.

The 450SL came with a three-speed automatic transmission, replacing the four-speed automatic used in the 350SL. A limited-slip differential was optional.

Like most Mercedes-Benz cars, the 450SL's brake pads create a great deal of dust. The pads are made soft in order to allow the driver to stop the car in case the power-assist unit fails. You can easily substitute hard pads to reduce or eliminate dust. Do not use the so-called brake dust shields to prevent dust on the wheels. Mercedes-Benz does not recommend these be used, as they restrict the amount of cooling air to the brakes. This increases brake fluid tempera-

★★★★   **450SLC 5.0**
★★★   **350SL, 350SLC, 450SL, 380SL, 500SL, 450SLC, 380SLC,**
            500SLC, 450SEL 6.9, 380SEC and 500SEC
★   **380SE and European 450SE, 450SEL, 500SE, 500SEL**

Continuing in the series of removable hardtop coupe roadsters was the 350SL, a misnomer in that it used a 4.5 liter engine rather than the 3.5 liter engine (which the designation implied). To confuse matters more, the 350SL in Europe used the 3.5 liter engine. (Mercedes-Benz)

In 1972, the 350SL was renamed 450SL — but not much but the name was changed. As sports cars go, the 450SL was quite heavy but still a great sports car. The option of using the soft top or hardtop made it all-season. (Mercedes-Benz)

ture and lowers the point of brake fade. (Incidentally, be careful around brake dust. Most brake pads contain asbestos, a suspected carcinogen, so do not inhale the dust, and wear gloves. "Dustless" brake pads are also available, which keep your wheels much cleaner and do not contain asbestos.)

Other weak points of the 450SL are the air conditioning, the water pump and the automatic climate control servo.

350SLC and 450SLC, 1971-80

The SLC models were stretched SLs made to accommodate four adults. The wheelbase was increased by about fourteen inches, with all of the extra length put into the area between the doorjam and the rear wheels. The 450SLC was about 175 pounds heavier than the 4,600 pound 450SL. The SLC's top was not removable, but a sunroof was available.

The new designation SLC stood for super light coupe. It has a fitting top, with ample room for two adults in the rear seat, easily recognized by its stylish rear window louvers. (Mercedes-Benz)

450SL: As attractive with the top up as down, its only visual sore spot was the large American DOT safety bumpers, which the European version was spared. European version also had single rectangular headlamps. (Mercedes-Benz)

It is interesting to note that during its production, the SLC was the highest-priced car in the Mercedes line, with the exception of the special-order 600. This fact always has a positive influence on appreciation potential of a car.

380SL, 1980-

In 1980, Mercedes introduced the 380SL (and 500SL in Europe), with a new, more streamlined body style. The 380 and 500SL used the same body but had different engine displacements, 3.8 and five liters, respectively. The 1986 models mark the sixteenth year of the very successful V-8 SL series.

The lighter-alloy V-8 of these new 380 and 500 SLs removed about 100 pounds from the front wheels, resulting in somewhat better handling as well as lower emissions. The 700 cc drop in displacement did not noticeably affect performance in comparison with the 450SL, which had the heavier engine. The 380SL enjoyed a long and happy life until the much-faster 560SL was introduced in 1986.

Despite its aged design, the SL maintained a steady popularity as a boulevardier, but in comparison with the similarly priced Porsche 928, its only advantage was that the top could be lowered. The collector potential of the 380SL is presently low; however, a well-kept example will always be valuable.

380SE, 380SEL and 380SEC, 1979-

For 1981, Mercedes-Benz replaced the 450SE/SEL with the 380SE/SEL in a completely new S-class bodyshell, the W 126 chassis. The car also had a new engine, the all-alloy M 116 3.8 liter V-8.

Although it was a more civilized and updated version of the flagship 450SEL, the 380SEL somehow didn't have its predecessor's appeal, especially when buyers knew the 500 version was being sold in Europe. Power was down to 155 hp, and when they

The 380SL interior was very clean and functional, with the traditional, firm Mercedes leather upholstery. (Mercedes-Benz)

The 450SLC was the most costly of the 450 series. It was a cross between the 450SL and the 450SE. It used the SL-style radiator grille with room for four adults. Again, it was quickly spotted by its rear window louvers. (Mercedes-Benz)

saw the $45,000 price tag, many potential buyers turned to the gray market to get more for their money.

Nevertheless, the 380SE/SEL was an excellent car, just not an enthusiast's car. Although slower than the 450SE/SEL, it got roughly ten percent better fuel mileage and boasted dozens of other improvements. One distinctive change (not an improvement) was the installation of a Becker Grand Prix electronic radio, the only original equipment radio available. This overpriced ($1,600), overcomplicated, underperforming accessory was universally panned. The same radio afflicts all other late-model US Mercedes-Benzes.

The 380SEC coupe was available only during the 1982 and 1983 model years, replaced in 1984 by the 500SEC. This sleek coupe has the distinction of being the first non-SL to scrap the traditional upright egg-crate grille in favor of the sleeker SL grille. The 380SE sedan continued through the 1984 model year as a more economical alternative to the 500SEL.

The 380SE/SEL/SECs seem to be very dependable cars with few problems. Beyond the poor radio, sometimes ineffective air conditioning (shared by most recent Mercedes-Benz cars) and a lack of power, only the power window mechanisms bring occasional complaints. The 380s can be expected to depreciate in value faster than the 500s because they are simply less desirable.

Late model

Mercedes-Benz's late-model V-8s are among the most durable and usable cars ever built. The 450 series set new standards, combining performance with comfort and dependability. Later, the 380 V-8s took this a step further, meeting the challenge of re-

380SL: The 3.8 liter engine in the new body line of the 1980s. A truly fun car to drive, with quality-crafted detail. (Mercedes-Benz)

strictive government regulations. Some might complain that the late-model sedans don't have as much wood (or character—there seems to be a relationship there) as the old Mercedes-Benz sedans, but the new cars still set the standard for all automakers.

The two most serious problems to look for in all of these cars are rust and accident damage. Should you find these problems on a car you are considering, keep in mind that most of these models are not rare, so there is likely a better car available. Another critical item on these expensive and complicated cars is regular maintenance. Most owners keep a complete maintenance record, and you should ask to see it. If no records are available, be very careful; parts and service are expensive.

A common problem on the 1977-80 cars is the automatic climate control servo, which frequently leaks or sticks, causing the heating/air conditioning to malfunction. This delicate servo is the central control point of the system, which brings together coolant, electrical and vacuum connections. The system was originally used in Chrysler cars and was made for DBAG in the United States. Its

The 227 hp Mercedes-Benz 560SL comes with a limited-slip differential, rear axle torque compensation device, ABS antilock brake system and a functional front air dam. Leather uphol-stery and an antitheft alarm are standard, as are the removable steel hardtop and fold-away soft top. Note change of wheel style. (Mercedes-Benz)

With the top down, the 560SL continued the great SL line. New-style alloy wheels added to the strong aerodynamic appearance. (Mercedes-Benz)

plastic center section is prone to cracking, which causes leaks. If such a leak is undetected, enough coolant can be lost to cause engine overheating and eventual seizing.

Mercedes-Benz makes a kit to replace the plastic section, and an aluminum center piece is available on the aftermarket. The servo also has other, more expensive, failure consequences requiring total replacement with a new or rebuilt unit. The latter is not available from dealers. This problem is not only peculiar to the V-8s, but is common to all 1977-80 models using the automatic climate control system.

450SE and 450SEL, 1972-80

The most significant sedan of the 1970s was the 450SE/SEL, which was introduced in 1973. Over 100,000 of these sedans were built before production ended in 1980. Since the 450s were so successful when new, there are plenty of these luxury cars available today, and you should have no trouble finding a good example at a fair price. As a highway car, the 450 is hard to beat, and it is surprisingly agile in corners as well. The 450s featured four-wheel disc brakes and a three-speed automatic transmission.

The SE and SEL differed in length by about 100 mm, with the SEL getting a larger rear seat/rear door area and longer wheelbase. The SEL was also about eighty pounds

heavier than the SE, but the extra weight did not affect performance (eighty pounds is not much in a two-ton car). European 450s ran 0-60 in about ten seconds and had a top speed of 130 mph; US versions were just a bit slower at 10.2 seconds and 127 mph.

The 450SE/SEL engine featured mechanical fuel injection and transistorized ignition. This was a dependable engine, but it can, like most other Mercedes-Benz engines, be a victim of valve guide wear and worn camshafts. The best way to detect cam wear is to remove the valve covers and carefully check each cam lobe for scoring, pitting or other failure of the heat treatment. Another fairly common problem with pre-1981 V-8s was water pump failure. Other than the above, these engines are trouble free and highly dependable.

Most of these cars are equipped with vacuum door locking, which can suffer various leaks caused by worn diaphragms. Replacement diaphragms are available in the aftermarket.

450SEL 6.9, 1975-80

In 1974, Mercedes introduced the mighty 450SEL 6.9, an enlarged version of the successful 450SEL. The new car featured more creature comforts and seventy more horsepower but a nearly identical body. The European version was able to move its 4,400

The 450SE 1972-80 was four inches shorter than the SEL. The difference was easy to spot in the length of the rear doors. (Mercedes-Benz)

pounds 0-60 in under eight seconds and had a top speed of 140 mph.

Mercedes produced 7,380 of the 450SEL 6.9s between 1975 and 1980, with the highest production, 1,839 units, coming in 1979.

This car must be rated as a future collectible. However, few 6.9s were officially imported to the United States. Many European 6.9s have been brought in (as used cars) through outside channels, so there are quite a few in America. This is partly because of price (over $38,000 in 1977, rising to over $50,000 by 1979, its last year).

When inspecting any European-version Mercedes-Benz, be aware that the car has probably seen hard use, and may have been improperly converted to US specifications. Also, resale value of European versions is considerably more variable than that of their US counterparts.

If you are looking for a good example, don't expect to find a neglected car at a low price and fix it up. Given the high cost of restoration, you would be better off finding the best example you can afford. If you want to get the most for your dollar, look at the

---

TYPE: 450SE/450SEL/450SL/450SLC

ENGINE

Type	V-8 overhead camshaft
Bore x stroke	3.62x3.35 in
Displacement	275.8 cu in
Valve operation	single overhead cam, chain driven
Compression ratio	8.0:1
Fuel system	fuel injection
Horsepower	180@4750 rpm
Torque	220@3000 rpm

CHASSIS & DRIVETRAIN

Clutch	single dry-plate
Transmission	3-speed automatic
Rear suspension	independent, diagonal swing axle, antilift control
Rear axle ratio	3.07:1
Front suspension	independent, double wishbones, antidive control

GENERAL

Wheelbase	450SE, 112.8; 450SEL, 116.7; 450SL, 96.9; 450SLC, 111.0
Track, front/rear	450SE, 59.9/59.3; 450SEL, 59.9/59.3; 450SL, 57.2/56.7; 450SLC, 57.2/56.7
Brakes	disc
Steering ratio	450SE, 2.7; 450SEL, 2.7; 450SL, 3.0; 450SLC, 3.0
Wheels	14 in steel disc
Tire size, front and rear	205x14 steel-belted radial
Maximum speed	5800 rpm
Gas tank capacity	450SE, 25.4 ltr; 450SEL, 25.4; 450SL, 23.8; 450SLC, 23.8 (3.4 gal reserve)

The 450SEL 6.9 had the same body as the 450SEL with an additional 2.4 liters of displacement. Selling in the high teens to mid-twenties, this car offers a lot for the money. (*Road & Track*)

Magnificent engine crammed into the 450SEL made enough muscle to frighten many a domestic sedan. *(Road & Track)*

The 450SEL was a great road car somewhat wasted on American roads. In Germany they are very comfortable cruising at 120 mph. (Tim Parker)

450SEL long body: Because these cars were built with very high standards, they make excellent transportation as used cars. (Mercedes-Benz)

6.3, but if you want luxurious performance, the 6.9 may be the car for you.

500SE, 500SEL, 500SEC and 500SL, 1979-

The 500SEL and SEC were first officially imported into the United States in 1984, even though they had been sold for many years in Europe. These cars formed the basis for the Mercedes-Benz gray market as we know it. The gray market brought models to the United States that otherwise would not have appeared, kept prices from rising and finally forced Mercedes-Benz of North America (MBNA) to bring in the big-engined cars.

The first 500SELs and SECs available in the United States were but pale shadows of the European versions, with their engines detuned from 230 to 180 hp. The 500SL was never available in the United States except as a 1985 model, but like other 500 sedans and coupes, many European 500SLs found their way into the United States. In 1986, the 500 sedan and coupe were replaced by the 420SE and the 560SEL/SEC. Also in 1986, the US version of the SL finally received a higher displacement and power, becoming the 560SL with 238 hp.

When shopping for these cars, performance (or lack of it) doesn't always matter as much as the "500" on the trunk lid. If you are looking for a near-new US model, try to make it a 1985 or later car. These cars are desired because of three very special letters:

ABS. These stand for antiskid braking system, a system first fitted to European models in 1978, but only recently available in the United States. This feature prevents the wheels from locking under braking, which benefits both steering and braking. This system is so impressive, once you have tried it, you will never want to be without it. ABS is standard equipment on the 1985 500SEC, 500SEL, 380SL, 380SE, 300SD and on most later models.

5.6 liter, 1985-

Mercedes-Benz of North America imported the 5.6 liter V-8 (M 117) in the 560SEL/SEC and 560SL for the 1986 model year. This was largely in response to growing demand for more power and in an effort to lessen the effects of the gray market. The 5.6 liter's 238 hp (compared with the 184 of the US 500) significantly improved performance giving the SEL and SEC a 0-60 mph time of eight seconds and a top speed of 140 mph. The cars also had a limited-slip differential and a hydropneumatic level control on the rear axle. And most of the US models

The back seat of the 500SEL was very roomy and very comfortable. The upholstery was hard by American car standards but orthopedically excellent. (Mercedes-Benz)

Current trend to blacken everything is only partially successful on this 450SEL shot in Pebble Beach, California, in 1986. (Tim Parker)

finally got the flush-faced halogen headlights with washers and wipers.

The 560SL had slightly reduced horsepower (228) because of a different exhaust system, but performance was about equal to the 560SEL/SEC.

European version

Americans have never been able to enjoy the pleasures of the European versions of the W 107 chassis, except by special importation. These cars include the 280SL, 280SLC (using the twin-cam six), 380SLC, 450SLC 5.0, 500SL (except in 1985) and 500SLC.

The most desirable of these cars is undoubtedly the 450SLC 5.0, built from 1977 to 1980. The 5.0 was the first to use the M 117 engine, putting out 240 DIN hp, with a top speed of 140 mph. The aluminum-alloy

The 500 SEC was certainly one of the great cars of all times—great performance, great ride, great comfort. It even handed you your seat belt shoulder strap and if you didn't want it, it retracted. The value system has changed since the SSK but for the 1980s, the 500SEC was a great car. (Mercedes-Benz)

In 1986, the 420SEL and 560SEL used the same coachworks. Increased aerodynamically over the 450SEL, the fluting has been removed from the lower belt molding of the 500SEL. (Mercedes-Benz)

engine (shared with the 500SL) was more than a modified 450 block. Many internal modifications made the lighter engine much stronger. This, combined with the aluminum hood and trunk lids, put the 5.0 about 220 pounds under the 450SLC. The 5.0 model is easily distinguished by its badge and front and rear spoilers.

In the 1970s, DBAG began selling the 5.0 liter cars in Europe, and it was not long

Cleaner, smoother, even less gaudy—the 560SEL is a bahnstormer of no mean repute. (Tim Parker)

560SEC: another super car. Sports car handling with luxury car comfort. (Mercedes-Benz)

before Americans learned about these models and lusted after them. The 500s were some of the most popular cars on the gray market up to 1984, when they finally became available as US models. So, although the 500s were not officially imported by MBNA until 1984, it was not difficult to find a 500SL, SEL, SEC or even SLC in the United States.

MBNA reluctantly began importing the 500SEL and SEC in 1984 in response to customer demand. Its reluctance was due to the effect the cars had on its Corporate Average Fuel Economy figures, as both cars easily qualified for the gas guzzler tax. The 500SL was not imported because the DBAG reportedly could not find a suitable place to mount the catalytic converter. However, a flow of 500SLs continued through the gray market.

The rarest of this group is the 500SLC, which formed the basis for the Mercedes-Benz rally team of the seventies. The car's aluminum-alloy engine offered some impressive performance characteristics.

As impressive as these cars sound, remember that most of these models were also brought into the United States as used cars. Again, they were *very* used. You're going to invest a lot of money in one of these cars, not just in purchase but in proper maintenance, so be careful. If you don't feel totally comfortable examining the car, take it to a Mercedes-Benz dealer or independent mechanic and have it checked over. Also look for structural damage and repairs. Fresh undercoating may be a sign of repair and rust.

The European 450SLC 5.0 was the standard 450SLC with the new five-liter engine, which introduced the 500 series. (Mercedes-Benz)

Chapter 10

Twin-cam six-cylinder

280SE, 1967-72

The 280 model designation ranges over twenty years of production and twenty-three different models. It is therefore quite confusing. The following list may be an aid to clarifying the situation:

Production	Model	Description
1967-72	280S	single overhead cam, 6-cylinder, S=super*
1967-72	280SE	single overhead cam, SE=super injected*
1969-71	280SEL	single overhead cam, SEL=super injected long (wheelbase)*
1970-72	280SE	3.5 V-8, SE=super injected 3.5 liter*
1971-76	280	double overhead cam, 6-cylinder*
1971-76	280E	double overhead cam, 6-cylinder, E=injected
1971-76	280CE	double overhead cam, 6-cylinder, CE= coupe injected
1971-76	280C	double overhead cam, C=coupe*
1971-72	280SE	4.5 V-8, SE=super injected 4.5 liter*
1971-72	280SEL	4.5 V-8, SEL=super injected long 4.5 liter*
1972-80	280S	S=S class and/or super*
1972-80	280SE	double overhead cam, 6-cylinder, SE=S-class/super injected*
1973-80	280SEL	double overhead cam, 6-cylinder, SEL=S-class/super injected long
1974-	280SL	double overhead cam, 6-cylinder, SL=sports light
1974-81	280SLC	double overhead cam, 6-cylinder, SLC=sports light coupe
1975-81	280	double overhead cam, 6-cylinder
1975-	280E	double overhead cam, 6-cylinder, E=injected*

★★	280C coupe and 280CE coupe
★	All other sedans

TYPE: 280SE/280SEL/280SE (coupe and convertible)

ENGINE

Type . . . . 6-cyl overhead camshaft (M 130)
Bore x stroke . . . . 86.5x78.8 mm (3.41x3.10 in)
Displacement . . . . 2778 cc (169.5 cu in)
Valve operation . . . . single overhead cam, chain driven
Compression ratio 9.5:1
Fuel system . . . . Bosch six-plunger pump
Horsepower . . . . 160 hp (DIN) @5500 rpm
Torque . . . . 24.5 mkg@4250 rpm

CHASSIS & DRIVETRAIN

Clutch . . . . single dry-plate
Transmission . . . . 4-speed manual and automatic
Rear suspension . . . . independent, coil springs, diagonal-pivot swing axle, antisway bars
Rear axle ratio 3.92
Front suspension . . . . independent front
Frame . . . . unit frame and body

GENERAL

Wheelbase . . . . 2750 mm (108.3 in); SEL, 2850 mm (112.2 in)
Track, front/rear . . . . 1482/1490 mm (58.4/58.7 in)
Brakes . . . . disc
Steering ratio 21.4:1
Wheels . . . . 14 in steel disc
Tire size, front and rear . . . . 7.35 H 14 or 185 H 14
Weight . . . . 1486 kg (3270 lb) SEL, 3305 lb; coupe, 3330 lb; convertible, 3495 lb
Maximum speed . . . . 190 km/h (118 mph); automatic, 185 km/h (115 mph)
Acceleration . . . . 10.5 sec 0-100 km/h
Fuel consumption . . . . 12.5 ltr, super/100 km (18.75 mpg)
Gas tank capacity . . . . 82 ltr (21.7 gal)

Production	Model	Description
1977-	280TE	double overhead cam, 6-cylinder, TE=station wagon injected
1978-81	280CE	double overhead cam, 6-cylinder, C=coupe injected*
1979-81	280S	double overhead cam, 6-cylinder, S=S-class/super*
1979-81	280	SE and SEL double overhead cam, 6-cylinder, SEL=S-class/super injected long*
1976-80	280C	double overhead cam, 6-cylinder, C=coupe

*Sold in the United States

Of this broad array, eight models are twin-cam sixes and were sold in the United States. The most desirable to the collector are the 1971-76 280C and 1976-80 280CE.

Much of the confusion can be cured by noticing that from 1967, 280S designates a

The advanced styling of the 15-year-old design of the 280C is very clear. Like all coupes, it has good collector potential. (Mercedes-Benz)

single overhead cam 6-cylinder, and from 1972 to the present 280S designates S-class body type. For example, the 1972-80 280SE uses the S-class body type common to the full range of S-class cars 1972 to the present. The 1971-76 280CE or 280E uses the earlier square-line body type.

The twin-cam 280's distinctive ribbed valve cover first appeared in the United States in carbureted form in the 1971 280C coupe. Sadly, the US version of the M 110 engine was restricted by emissions, and power dropped from the European version's 160 hp to 120. Production of the carbureted car ended in 1976, and the United States got fuel-injected versions of the 1976 280E se-

dan and the 1978 280SE coupe. None of these models were produced in large numbers, making them interesting to the collector.

280C, 1971-76

The 1971 280C coupe was Mercedes' first US twin-cam six-cylinder engine. The body, based on the W 114 sedan, had also been used for the 250C which had the single-cam six. The 280C's carbureted engine was saddled with emission controls and produced only 120 hp, considerably less than the 185 hp European versions.

The Solex 4A1 four-barrel carburetor of the 280C (and 280 sedan) does not have a

The 280CE outpaces its carbureted sibling, the 280C, in performance and collectibility. Note change of bodyshell compared with the earlier 280C. (Mercedes-Benz)

The 300E started production in 1986. It is a totally new model, high tech, and extremely aerodynamic along with having light weight. It comes with ABS antilock braking system as standard equipment along with antitheft alarm system, halogen headlights, central locking and tachometer just to mention a few items. This car goes like a rocket, which belies its sedate looks. (Mercedes-Benz)

sterling reputation; as with any other carburetor, age and wear take their toll. However, properly updated and tuned, it can give excellent performance. Carburetor update kits are available and include different jets and a modified accelerator pump. The second stage should be set to open as early as possible, and the shifting rods can be adjusted so the shifts happen at higher rpm.

The coupes seem to be more subject to window-raising problems than the sedan version. The problem lies in faulty limit switches which can cause the electric motors to overrun, possibly damaging the door structure.

280CE, 1978-81

The 280CE coupe replaced the old W 114-based 280C coupe with a completely new body based on the new W123 sedan. This car was sold in the United States from 1978 through the 1981 model year. Bosch K-Jetronic fuel-injection put the engine's output at nearly 140 hp, depending on year and version (the California version had 137 hp). The same body was shared by the 300CD, the turbo-diesel-powered equivalent, but fewer 280CEs were sold in the United States.

When comparing the coupe versions of earlier cars such as the 220S/SE with these

300CD turbo coupe. Although it is a high-production car, its line and performance will make it collectible. (Tim Parker)

models, the 280C/CE represents fair collector potential.

280 and 280E, 1971-81

The 280 sedan used the same engine as the 280C and therefore suffered from the same lack of power. The 280 was sold in the United States as a 1976 model, but was replaced in 1977 by the more successful, fuel-injected 280E. The 280E offers the best performance of these late-model six-cylinder sedans because it used the mid-range body instead of the full-size sedan body of the 280S/SE. The 280E, voted 1977 Import Car of the Year by *Motor Trend* magazine, produced about 140 hp and came with a four-speed automatic transmission. Production lasted through the 1981 model year.

280S and 280SE, 1978-81

In response to the energy crisis in the United States, Mercedes introduced the 280S

TYPE: 280

ENGINE

Type	6-cyl overhead camshaft (M 110)
Bore x stroke	86x78.8 mm (3.40x3.10 in)
Displacement	2746 cc (169.5 cu in)
Valve operation	single overhead cam, chain driven
Compression ratio	9:1
Fuel system	Bosch six-plunger pump
Horsepower	160 hp (DIN) @5500 rpm
Torque	23 mkg@4000 rpm

CHASSIS & DRIVETRAIN

Clutch	single dry-plate
Transmission	4-speed manual and 5-speed manual and automatic
Rear suspension	independent, coil springs, diagonal-pivot swing axle, antisway bars
Rear axle ratio	3.69
Front suspension	independent front
Frame	unit frame and body

GENERAL

Wheelbase	2750 mm (108.3 in); SEL, 2850 mm (112.2 in)
Track, front/rear	1444/1440 mm (56.9/56.7 in)
Brakes	disc
Steering ratio	21.4:1
Wheels	14 in steel disc
Tire size, front and rear	7.35 H 14 or 185 H 14
Weight	1455 kg (3200 lb)
Maximum speed	190 km/h (118 mph); automatic, 185 km/h (115 mph)
Acceleration	13 sec 0-100 km/h
Fuel consumption	12.5 ltr, super/100 km (18.75 mpg)
Gas tank capacity	65 ltr (17.2 gal)

and 280SE sedans. These shared the S-class W 116 body of the formidable 450SE. This was a problem in the 1974-76 280S because its 120 hp would not perform very well in the 3,900 pound car. The 140 hp fuel-injected 280SE, produced from 1977 to 1979, did not perform much better. Frankly, these cars, especially encumbered with automatic transmission, are slow and are best regarded as fuel-saving alternatives to the thirstier V-8.

The 280S and 280SE shared many of the amenities of the 450SE, but they were hindered by the needs to meet emission standards and get the best possible gas mileage. These cars were quite popular in Europe but relatively uncommon in the United States.

European twin-cam six

Although 1981 marked the last year the United States would see the M 110 twin-cam six-cylinder, several versions continued to be available in Europe. One such model was the 280SE/SEL sedan. This car was based on the 450SE's W 116 body produced from 1973 to 1980, and was updated to the W 126 body in 1980. The European 280SE engine produced more power (185 hp) than the US

version of the 500 (174 hp). The optional manual transmission made the 280SE exciting to drive. Although never imported by MBNA, this late-model gasoline six-cylinder may be found on the gray market.

The 280SL and 280SLC were never offi-

Distinctive rear end of the 300E; note angled trunk sides. Relatively unimpressive to look at, but a mover and a shaker on the street. (Tim Parker)

Modified 300E with spoilers, skirts, wheels and tires. A wonderful modern GT four-seater. (Tim Parker)

cially imported, but are excellent cars. Production began in 1974, and the 280SL was built through 1985 (280SLC production ceased in 1981). Both models are equipped with the M 110, 185 hp engine, which compares favorably in output with the US V-8 versions. The optional five-speed manual transmission makes these cars even more delightful to drive than the European 280SE sedan. Beginning in 1986 the six-cylinder 300SL was available as a European model with the new single-cam six.

MBNA has never imported the 280TE gasoline-powered station wagon, but this 185 hp six-cylinder has been popular in Europe since 1977. Some of these wagons were imported privately and if you look long and hard enough, you'll find one. Those with the hydropneumatic rear level control are more desirable.

300E, 1984-

Mercedes-Benz did not import any six-cylinder cars to the United States from 1982 through 1985. In 1986, Mercedes introduced a new six-cylinder, the M 103, in the new 300E mid-range sedan (W 124). This 2.8 liter single-cam engine was lighter than the old M 110, but had a deeper, more rigid cast-iron block. The Bosch KE-III mechanical fuel injection with electronic correction and the microprocessor-controlled ignition produced 177 hp.

The 300E was a completely new car. The new engine, lighter body and better aerodynamics gave this car an honest top speed of 140 mph. The rear suspension incorporated the five-link system first seen in the 190 series. Transmission included the four-speed automatic and a five-speed manual, the latter being relatively rare.

Chapter 11

Daily drivers

Sedans offer quite a variety of good points and bad points. Whether or not you consider a sedan will depend on your particular expectations and opinions.

Sedans are practical cars, produced in large numbers. This means that they are less expensive than sportier models and are easier to locate. Sedans are also less expensive to restore since they used steel body framing rather than the wood of earlier convertibles. However, you cannot afford to spend much on restoration if you expect to get any return on your investment. Since there is little appreciation on a sedan from un-

The 180/190 body style with the sportiest option available — the full sunroof. If found in good original condition with low mileage and a history of maintenance, these cars are good economical transportation. (Mercedes-Benz)

★★	**Diesel coupes**
★	**All sedans**

restored to restored condition, you are better off finding the most complete and correct original car for your money.

If the coupes and cabriolets of the fifties are among the most desired cars, the sedans

The 180 and 190 series cars are easy to maintain but be very careful of rust in the unibody construction. Restoration cost can easily be more than the car's restored value. (Mercedes-Benz)

The 220S is a definite modernization over its predecessor the 220. This puts it on a difficult middle ground — not new enough for general daily use but not classic enough for strong collectibility.

of the same era must be the most overlooked Mercedes-Benz collectibles. Their collectibility is not necessarily monetarily justified. However, their charm can be the source of much pleasure.

In the mid-fifties, Mercedes introduced an electric clutch called the Hydrak. This system worked quite well when the car was new, but age and mileage take their toll on the Hydrak's operation. If you are considering a car with the Hydrak clutch, make sure it works properly. Maintenance and adjustment information is available on these clutches, and they can also be converted to the standard mechanical system.

Check these sedans over thoroughly, as rust can start in many places. Particularly look under the floor mats, the battery shelf, inner fender panels behind the headlights and the bottoms of the fenders and trunk floor. Also check the rear swing-axle boots for leaks.

Heater valves on these sedans are usually stuck, but they can be freed and repaired easily. The accompanying heater air ducts on either side of the engine compartment are also frequently in need of repair.

1960s sedans

The sedan versions of the 180, 190, 220 A,

The 300SE body differs from the 220 models only in the addition of wheel opening trim. Otherwise, the highline fin-style cars are basically alike. The wide whitewall tire on this factory photo reinforces the idea that these cars were directed at the American market. (Mercedes-Benz)

The 220b: Although dated in design, there are bargains to be had for transportation. (Mercedes-Benz)

219, 220SSE and 300 models featured quite pleasing body styles and were generally very reliable with good availability of spare parts.

Here's the "fin" with chrome bezel—must be highline, and just right for the American market of the day. (Tim Parker)

The 190, 200, 220Sb-SEb, 230Sb and 300SEb sedans of the early sixties all used the same basic body. Although these models were very reliable, it takes a real dedication to love their American-influenced finned rear fenders.

1970s sedans

Mercedes-Benz offered some outstanding sedans in the early seventies, but as the decade waned, so did the cars. The 6.3, introduced in 1968, was a superb car, but by 1980, diesel sedans had assumed a large share of Mercedes-Benz sales in the United States.

The seventies are a confusing period for Mercedes-Benz followers. The W 109 body, which appeared in the late sixties, offered six different engine options—three six-cylinders and three eight-cylinders—all during a four-year period.

After 1972, the 280S/SE sedans used the twin-cam six-cylinder. The 3.5 and 4.5 V-8s were also used in the W-bodied 280SE 3.5,

Differentiated from the highline fin style by its single headlights, the lowline fin-style value is as practical transportation or, in some cases, sentimental. (Mercedes-Benz)

280SE 4.5, 300SE 3.5 and 300SE 4.5. Aside from the engines, the main difference between these cars was the 280's use of conventional coil spring suspension and the 300's use of air suspension. The 280 and 300SEL 4.5s can be good buys for transportation, and you may be pleasantly surprised by their performance. However, do not expect good fuel economy—12 mpg was about average.

Modernization continues with a shorter and wider radiator shell for the highline six-cylinder. The fins of its predecessors turned out to be less prophetic than predictions led us to believe in the early sixties. (Mercedes-Benz)

The workhorse of their time, the squareline models were available with a wide range of engines. They are a definite consideration for daily transportation. The interior and mechanics are very durable and with minimum maintenance they can run for hundreds of thousands of miles. (Mercedes-Benz)

1980s sedans

The Mercedes sedans of the eighties are among the finest in the world. Still, many complain they have lost some of the appeal of the older models. True, there is not as much wood used on interior appointments, performance was down a bit until 1986, the air conditioning and climate control systems

Rear fin detail—relatively simple 280SE workhorse. (Tim Parker)

leave a bit to be desired, stereos are poor, the transmission could be smoother and they are expensive.

None of these complaints, however, detracts from a Mercedes-Benz when it comes to comfort, reliability, longevity, safety and retained value. The alloy 3.8 liter V-8 engine is as dependable as any engine ever built. Parts and service are commensurate with the car's purchase price.

Nearly three-quarters of all Mercedes sold in the United States during the 1980s were diesels, so your first decision in buying a late-model sedan is whether you want a diesel- or gasoline-fueled car. Making this decision is purely personal, and you will find almost militant advocates of each fuel. If you want a station wagon, you have no choice— only diesels have been imported.

There is no longer a drastic difference in performance between gasoline and diesel engines, since the addition of the turbocharger, which has proven to be quite reliable. If you are considering a normally aspirated diesel, drive it on the highway before you buy it. Acceleration can be slow and

The S-class sedan was the beginning of clear aerodynamic influence. They are totally modern vehicles; very dependable as daily transportation. (Mercedes-Benz)

even dangerous. The main advantage of the diesel is mechanical longevity, as there are no longer differences in fuel prices or maintenance costs.

The 1984 190 models are virtually trouble free, as are the 380SE, SEL and SECs. The late-model 500s again complain of air conditioning and climate control problems.

If you are looking for a newer US model Mercedes-Benz, try to make it a 1985 car, recommended because of the benefits of the ABS. The antiskid braking system was stan-

This short-body version is a 280SE with sunroof. The bumpers give away the fact that it is a European version. The wheelbase of the 280SE was approximately four inches shorter than that of the 450SEL. Generally speaking, the longer the wheelbase the greater the stability. But this is paid for by loss in maneuverability. (Mercedes-Benz)

Continuing the basic lines of the earlier 1967-76 squareline series, this series (1975-82) also offered a wide range of engines from the four-cylinder 200 to the six-cylinder 280E. The diesel is low maintenance and economical with fuel consumption. (Mercedes-Benz)

dard equipment on the 1985 500SEC, 500SEL, 380SL, 380SE and 300SD; an option on the 190E 2.3, and 190D 2.2; and was not available on the W 123 bodied 300CD, 300D or 300TD.

Diesels

Diesels are not usually considered collector cars, but since Mercedes popularized the diesel passenger car, they should not be overlooked. Daimler-Benz built and sold the first diesel passenger car, the model 206D, in 1936. However, it wasn't until after World War II that Mercedes reached full stride in diesel car production. During the 1950s, Mercedes-Benz slowly made the world aware of the practical uses of diesel-powered automobiles. These cars were well built and well maintained, and many of them still survive today.

More aerodynamic than the original S-class bodies, the second-stage S-class has a big improvement in the bumper design. With a wide range to choose from, this is an excellent place to look for a very durable and dependable used car. (Mercedes-Benz)

Uniqueness and rarity of the 230S station wagon make it interesting, especially to a collector.

The coachworks on this 230S station wagon looks factory, but it is a custom job.

Evolution of a sedan—top, second-series S;
right, first-series S class; left, 190E, a sort of
mini-S. (Mercedes-Benz)

300TD Turbo Diesel—A rare sight in the United
States, a factory station wagon. (Tim Parker)

Diesel models from the sixties can also still serve well as everyday transportation. Maintenance costs are generally lower than a gasoline-powered car, and diesel engines usually last longer.

Diesel-powered cars accounted for roughly seventy-five percent of all Mercedes-Benzes sold in the United States during the early 1980s. The main advantage was economy, but Daimler-Benz added another incentive, the turbocharger. Mercedes-Benz became the first turbocharged passenger car offered in the United States. The turbo dramatically improved performance and removed the last serious impediment of diesel ownership. In 1984, Mercedes-Benz introduced the trap oxidizer on some models. For the first time, diesels had a means to control smoke, particulates and odor.

The late-model turbocharged diesels are among the most popular Mercedes-Benz models in the United States. The turbodie-

The world's first production diesel car was the 1936 260D. Still not a big collector car, should you find one. (Mercedes-Benz)

The 1986's long-wheelbase 300SDL features a 148 hp turbo six-cylinder diesel, which has been encapsulated for noise reduction. Diesel power still moves it. It's doubtful we'll see long-term collectibility. (Mercedes-Benz)

sel's performance is far superior to the normally-aspirated diesels, at no extra cost in fuel mileage. The turbochargers are as reliable as the traditional diesel engines. The only operational drawback is making sure you use good-quality fuel. Contaminated or poor diesel fuel can clog injectors, allow algae to form in fuel tanks and turn to a gel in very cold weather. Additives are available to control condensation and algae, and engine block and fuel heaters help in cold climates.

In 1949, the 170D was introduced, and it continued in production through 1955. The engine was developed from the 1936 260D, the world's first diesel production car. The 170 four-cylinder diesel engine was offered in both the 170V and 170S four-door sedans.

Like the gasoline engines, as improvements were made, different designations were given to indicate the improvement. Therefore, the 170Da was introduced in 1950, the 170DS in 1952 and both the 170Db and 170S-D in 1953.

The 170D was available only in the four-door sedan. The early 170D, 170Da and 170Db used the 170V body and the 170DS and 170S-D used the 170S body. Generally, the values of the 170 diesels run the same as those of the like-bodied 170V and 170S models.

One reason for choosing the diesel over the gasoline 170 engine is the diesel's extreme ease of maintenance. The lack of a carburetor, spark plugs, ignition points and

Current "mini" diesel: the 190D 2.5 with 93 hp five-cylinder engine. It's faster than the pre-1986 190D 2.4 four. (Mercedes-Benz)

a secondary electrical system eliminates many common engine problems.

When examining one of these cars, all the rules that apply to the gasoline-engined 170 apply here as well. Be sure to drive a diesel version so that you have an idea of how the car performs.

Still called a 190 but the 1987 model 190D is up to 2.5 liters. The boost in horsepower is considerable. (Tim Parker)

What is this? 124 bodyshell but 2.4 and turbo? 1986 in California? Collectors, beware; not every car is what it appears. (Tim Parker)

Chapter 12

Modern 190

The introduction of the 190 series in 1982, built on the W 201 chassis, brought Mercedes-Benz into a younger, more enthusiast oriented marketplace. Shortly after its introduction as a US model in 1984, the 190 became the most popular car in Mercedes' US line-up.

In 1983 Mercedes-Benz introduced the modestly sized 190D 2.2 and 190E 2.3 as US models for 1984. The 190E was the vanguard of a new generation of more efficient, higher-performance Mercedes-Benz sedans. The diesel 190D and the gasoline 190E shared an ingenious new five-link rear suspension design that allowed them to handle better than any previous Mercedes production car.

Shortly after the 190's introduction, DBAG announced the 190E 2.3-16. This car featured a sixteen-valve head design, developed in conjunction with Cosworth Engineering. The 1985 European model of the

The 1982 190E with a 1.9 liter diesel or gasoline engine. The 190E is fuel injected, and the straight 190 used one Stromberg carburetor.

This was Mercedes' first drop below 2.0 liters since 1965 with the discontinuation of the 190c. (Mercedes-Benz)

| ★★ | 190E 2.3-16 |
| ★ | All sedans |

2.3-16 boasted 185 hp and even outperformed the 5.0 liter S-class cars! By 1986 the sixteen-valve car was available in 167 hp US trim and, thanks to various differences, performance nearly matched the European models.

While DBAG made great strides in developing this new series, it also went to great pains to ensure the car retained its identity as a Mercedes-Benz. Despite the radically new and downsized exterior, the 190's interior is nearly identical to that of larger models, and the familiar grille was retained, as well.

The 190 series has proven to be popular and reliable. The majority of owners report no major problems with the cars. There have been only a few complaints about hardshifting with the automatic transmission, difficult shifting with the manual transmission, and problems with the air conditioning and the electric window lifts.

If you are prepared to spend $20,000 for a used Mercedes-Benz, consider a 190. Apart from a lack of rear-seat legroom, these cars match the old 300D models (W 123) series in interior space, but more important, they outperform their predecessors in every area. The five-link rear suspension is the best rear suspension ever installed in a Mercedes. The car remains stable under heavy cornering and even heavy braking. An experienced driver will find it more forgiving than the old swing-axle or trailing arm rear suspension systems.

If you are looking for a newer-model 190, try to find a 1985 car. Again, this is because of the antiskid braking system introduced

The new 1986 190E with a 16 valve 2.3 fuel-injected engine. Very aerodynamic and excellent at high speed, as proved in an endurance test in 1983. The 190E averaged 154.06 mph over 31,000 miles, with a 0-60 time of less than eight seconds and a top speed of 156 mph. Impressed? If not, you should be! (Mercedes-Benz)

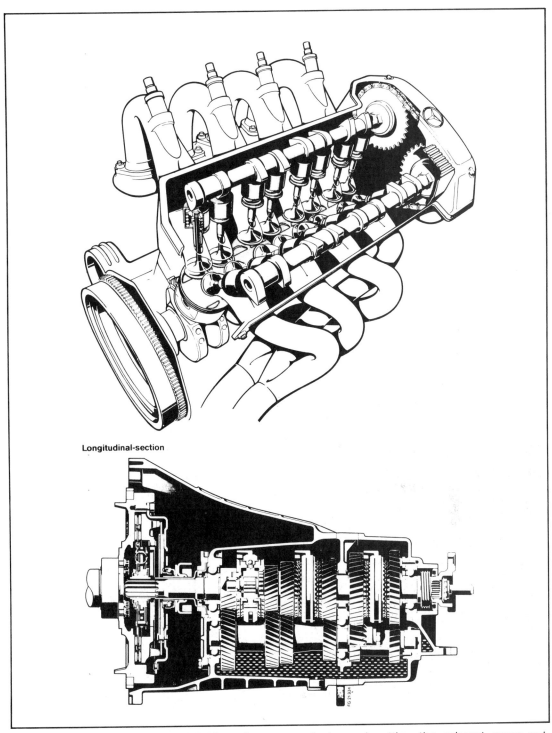

Longitudinal-section

The 16 valve, twin cam 190E 2.3-16 engine; exhaust on one cam, intake on the other. It's a matter of getting more air/gas mixture into the cylinder and getting the exhaust gases out. (Mercedes-Benz)

that year. The Mercedes-Benz Supplementary Restraint System (an airbag on the driver's side, a tightening seat belt on the front passenger side) was also optional on the 1984 and 1985 190s and became standard for 1986.

The first update of the 190 series came in January 1985, when the cars got a new articulated windshield wiper. The single wiper operated on a gear, allowing it to sweep eighty-six percent of the windshield. Fifteen-inch wheels became standard for both the 190D and 190E at the same time. The 190 series also suffered its first recall in 1985, based on the possibility of cracks in the fourteen-inch alloy wheels. These wheels had date codes between 3583 and 4983.

190E 2.3 and 2.6, 1983-

In 1984, the 113 hp 190E 2.3 was capable of a top speed of 120 mph and still delivered over 30 mpg. It was the first Mercedes-Benz to demonstrate the new low-drag, low-weight technology that led to higher performance. For 1985, the 190E was beefed up to 120 hp with a newly designed intake manifold. The center console was altered in 1986. For 1987 there was another model, the 190E 2.6, with a little more go.

The 190E 2.3 handles very well and has become quite popular and successful in club driving events. The aftermarket has developed a variety of high-performance equipment for the 190, including spoilers, alloy wheels, stiffer and shorter springs and even a turbocharger.

190D 2.2 and 2.5, 1983-

The 2.2 liter version of this car was for diesel fans only, while the later 2.5 liter version offered acceptable performance. The 190D easily outperformed the 240D but a 190D owner must be tolerant of slow acceleration, especially with the automatic trans-

This is a new form of information on the 190E trunk. It tells you this model has a 190 body, it is fuel injected and it is powered by a 2.3 liter engine using 16 valves. (The rear spoiler is standard.) (Tim Parker)

mission. Therefore, the five-speed manual gearbox is recommended. The highway fuel mileage of the 190D 2.2 was impressive, with frequent readings of 40 mpg and with 50 mpg very attainable. DBAG realized that American diesel owners wanted more performance, so in 1986 the 190D's engine was enlarged to five cylinders and 2.5 liters. These changes raised the horsepower from seventy-two to ninety-three.

The 190D was essentially identical to the 190E 2.3. The drop in popularity of the diesel in the mid-1980s meant the 2.2 version depreciated more rapidly than the other Mercedes cars, so some good bargains can be found.

190E 2.3-16, 1983-

The 190E 2.3-16, introduced in Germany in 1984, set dramatic new performance standards for modern American Mercedes-Benz cars. No doubt this model will become a collector item in the near future.

The 190 Sport, as it was sometimes called, was basically a factory high-performance version of the 190E 2.3. Its four-valves-per-cylinder head helped propel the car to an honest 140 mph. These 190s are a delight to drive—quick, nimble and fast, yet still comfortable, practical and tame.

In 1986, Americans were officially offered the 190 2.3-16, and the car was only slightly different than the European version. The US sixteen-valve's horsepower was knocked down to 167 from the European's 185 hp. However, the American car got a lower rear axle ratio, which meant only slightly diminished acceleration. The US version also had a slightly lower compression ratio, even though the heads were the same as those on the European model. This resulted in a 9.7:1 ratio in US models versus 10.5:1 in European models. The American 2.3-16 was offered with either the Getrag five-speed manual transmission or the Daimler-Benz four-speed automatic.

The 190E 2.3-16 had so many subtle improvements over the 190E 2.3 that it is worth the higher price to own a genuine car rather than a 190E that has been modified to perform like the 190 Sport. For example, the manual transmission is easier to shift, the brakes are larger and the suspension is modified for sportier driving. All US sixteen-valve cars have the ABS and the Supplementary Restraint system.

For 1986-87, the 190E 2.2 became the 2.3, which should make it more competitive with BMW's mid-range. There's a 2.6 too. (Tim Parker)

Chapter 13

Rare, desirable, unusual

The mystique of Mercedes-Benz, indeed much of the foundation of its commercial success, is based on a number of glorious racing cars and racing successes. These cars have always been very valuable, and very rare. Short of making a replica, there's little chance that one will come on the market. Occasionally those in private hands appear at vintage racing events. More infrequently, those cars still held by Mercedes-Benz are shown off, usually driven by their favored drivers—the likes of Hermann Lang, Juan Manuel Fangio and Stirling Moss.

The W-series cars—W-25, W-154 and W-154/163 of the 1930s and the W-196 of the mid-1950s—were designed purely as Grand Prix cars. All are stunning—looks, noise, performance. Factory sports-racing cars, such as the 300SLR of the same era as the W-196, are just as charismatic, just as rare, and nearly as valuable. Don't expect to find one on a used-car lot!

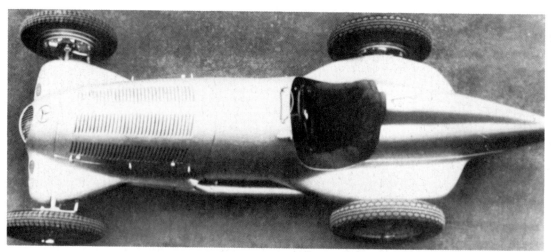

The 1934 W-25 was the first result of the huge amounts of money poured into the development of a super Mercedes racing machine by the Hitler propaganda machine. The W-25 eight-cylinder with a bore and stroke of 78x88 had a displacement of 3.36 liters producing 314 bhp at 5500 rpm. In 1936, the displacement was increased to 4.74 liters, boosting the bhp to 450 at 5800 rpm. (Mercedes-Benz)

New for 1937, the W-125 was truly a super racing machine. The W-25 chassis was lengthened by a foot, and the engine displacement was increased to 5.6 with a bhp output of 550 at 5800 rpm. It was capable, with its streamlined body, of average speeds on the Avus track in Berlin of 155 to 165 mph. (Mercedes-Benz)

W-125 just before its run at the Laguna Seca, California, vintage races in August 1986. Hermann Lang got well into the spirit with this car on that day. Can you buy one? Would it be the best M-B investment? (Tim Parker)

Demand for these cars has always been high. It will get higher as the revival of historic races, such as the Mille Miglia, proceeds. I expect their value to rise into the millions of dollars. Other special Mercedes, be they competition cars or those with custom bodies, must be looked at on an individual basis. Custom coachwork is valuable only when the styling is desirable; a rare car that is ugly is not likely to be sought after.

Over the years, numerous coachbuilders have created special-use or optional modifications on standard factory bodies. These have included station wagons, hearses, delivery vehicles and, more recently, a growing trend of "add on" spoilers and trim. If these modifications are professionally done and the styling is pleasant, they can be of value.

Only a small selection of what you might see on the street is shown here.

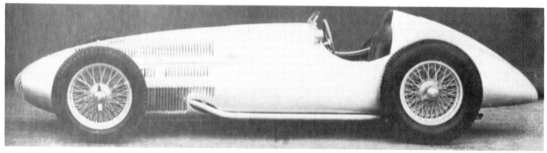

In 1939, Mercedes added a two-stage blower to the M-154 engine (V-12 three-liter of the 1938 W-154) and designated it the M-163. The coachwork was more streamlined, with 150 pounds pared off its predecessor. Power output was up 50 bhp, to 480 bhp at 7500 rpm. Its extremely successful career was cut short by the outbreak of World War II. (Mercedes-Benz)

In 1954, Mercedes re-entered Grand Prix racing for the first time since 1939. Its entry was the W-196 with a straight-eight, 12.5 liter fuel-injected engine. In its final development in 1955, it produced 280 bhp at 8500 rpm and won six out of seven Grand Prix races in 1955. In 1955, Mercedes chose to close its racing department and has not reopened it to this day. (Mercedes-Benz)

Imagine either Juan Manuel Fangio or Stirling Moss at these controls. How the shape of Grand Prix cars has changed in 30 years! Car not for sale. (Tim Parker)

Two-seater cockpit of the 300SLR similar to the one Moss and Jenkinson drove to victory in the Mille Miglia. Compare it with that of the W-196. (Tim Parker)

The 300SLR (for super light racing) was introduced in 1954 as a sports racing car. Its design owes more to the W-196 than its namesake, the 300SL. The eight-cylinder engine, with a square bore and stroke of 78x78 mm, had a displace-ment of three liters, with 300 hp at 7500 rpm. Top speed was 180 mph. Its racing successes were numerous, which included the 1955 Mille Miglia, the Targa Florio and the Irish TT. (Mercedes-Benz)

300SLR at Laguna Seca in 1986 during the vintage races at which Daimler-Benz celebrated its centenary. Moss drove this Mille Miglia style on the track and diced with Fangio aboard the W-196. Against factory orders, of course! (Tim Parker)

So-called replica doesn't fool anyone, or does it? Fiberglass and Ford make a nice enough car, especially when the real thing isn't available. (Tim Parker)

The real thing, in fact, but cars like this may arouse your suspicions at first. Be careful. A 300SL-based open two-seater sports-racing raced at the time at the East Coast tracks. Beautiful, useful and a reasonable investment potential. (Tim Parker)

Just after World War II, there were numerous special-bodied Mercedes, as indeed there were in the thirties. Literally dozens of prototypes were produced. Here's a 170D panel van made between 1951 and 1953—more fun potential than investment, perhaps. (Mercedes-Benz)

Again, not an investment by any stretch of the imagination but a good workhorse: 1967, seven-seat, 200D limousine. Many, many Mercedes are used as taxis, which may be a shock to many an American enthusiast. (Mercedes-Benz)

"Old" ambulances make good delivery wagons. This is a 1977 250/240D/300D chassis. Investment, no! (Mercedes-Benz)

Type 300 hearse built in 1955 by Lueg in Essen. Interesting to say the least, but is it a good investment? (Mercedes-Benz)

The C-111 that Daimler-Benz took to Laguna Seca for its centenary in 1986. It was impressive by its silent speed. Stirling Moss (white shirt and pants) peers in. (Tim Parker)

The C-111/11 is one of Mercedes-Benz' experimental cars in this series. This one is powered by a four-rotor Wankel rotary engine. It developed 187 mph, and 0-60 mph in 4.8 seconds. Not for sale, today. (Mercedes-Benz)

Custom-bodied 190E: expensive cabriolet work by Tuning-Schulz of Korschenbroich, West Germany. Typical of the smooth style of coachwork done by many companies in the 80s, with AMG being, perhaps, the best known and the master craftsman. (Mercedes-Benz)

Gelandewagen 230G, or GE, of 1982. It is shown here because none of this series of off-road vehicles can yet be considered investment material. Give it ten years, maybe. A cooperative effort with Steyr-Daimler-Puch of Austria, past masters of off-road ability, these gas- and diesel-powered vehicles came in both short- and long-wheelbase vehicles, and follow the Mercedes-Benz tradition started by the "truck division's" Unimog. (Mercedes-Benz)

It isn't close, but then it probably isn't intended
to be. Never mind the style, just feel the price!
(Tim Parker)

Someone loves this Rambler enough to make it a Mercedes-Benz; it was well executed, too. Doesn't Rambler-Benz sound appropriate? (Tim Parker)

Stretchers are a common sight in the modern city. This is 300E based and thus brand new in late 1986. Not what the designer had in mind with the original hot-shot 300E, though. (Tim Parker)

Model designations

Things get a bit more complicated here, but the system can still be deciphered. Upper-case letters have different meanings from lower-case letters. While it is impossible to generalize, here is a full list of letter suffixes and their meanings.

Upper-case letters

A: a two-door, two-passenger cabriolet or coupe, used up through the mid-1950s (220 cabriolet A or 220 coupe A); not used for current models

B: a similar cabriolet, but with rear seat and separate rear quarter windows to accommodate two or three more passengers (540K cabriolet B); also no longer used

C: in prewar cars, a two-door coupe or cabriolet body for four or five passengers with no rear quarter window; this designation is still used to indicate coupes (300CD, coupe, diesel)

D: diesel powered (240D)

TD: turbocharged diesel (300TD), or transport diesel (300TD wagon)

E: *einspritzer*, or fuel injected (280E)

G: *gelandewagen*, or off-road vehicle (280G)

H: *heck*, or rear; used to denote a rear-mounted motor in the prewar 130H and 170H

K: either *kurz*, short wheelbase (SSK or model K), or *kompressor*, supercharger (500K)

L: *licht*, or lightweight (190SL or SSKL), or *lang*, for long wheelbase (300SEL)

M: motor-type number (see the following chart)

S: sport or super; used to denote a sports model (190SL) or a slightly higher output (250S)

SS: super sport

T: transport or turbocharged

TD: transport, station wagon (300TD)

V: *vergaser*, carbureted (170V)

W: *wagen*, or chassis type (see the following chart)

Lower-case letters

a, b, c, or d: usually designate developments of an ongoing model; for example, the 300 first appeared as such, then became the 300a, 300b, 300c and 300d. Not to be confused with the upper-case letters.

Some typical model designations are as follows:

180	1.8 liter, gasoline-powered
180D	1.8 liter, diesel-powered
220SE	2.2 liter, fuel-injected
220SEb	2.2 liter, fuel-injected, newer body style
230SL	2.3 liter, sports light
280E	2.8 liter, fuel-injected
280SL	2.8 liter, sports light
280SE 3.5	3.5 liter, fuel-injected
280SE 4.5	4.5 liter, fuel-injected
290	2.9 liter, prewar car
300b	3.0 liter sedan, development of the 300
300SEL	3.0 liter, long wheelbase
300SEL 6.3	6.3 liter engine in the 300SEL body
380SEC	3.8 liter, fuel-injected coupe
450SLC	4.5 liter, sports light coupe

To further complicate things, M and W, designating motor and chassis types, respectively, are sometimes used. These are handy when interchanging parts common to different models using common bodies of engines. For example, the 300SEL and 300SEL 6.3 both have a W 109 body; the 380SEL and 380SL share the M 116 engine.

Chassis and engine numbers

The following chart is very handy for checking correct engine and chassis numbers. This is important since so many different engines were used in a variety of Mercedes-Benz chassis. You can also see the significance of the digits used in the two numbers.

Chassis (W)	Engine (M)	Model	Year
06	06	Type SS	1928-33
15	15	170	1931-36
22	22	380K	1933-34
24	24	500K	1934-36
28	28	170H	1936-39
29	29	540K	1936-40
100	100	600 sedan and Pullman	1963-81
105	180	219 sedan	1956-59
107 E45	117	450SL, 450SLC	
108 II	108	250S	1965-69
108 III	108	250SE sedan	1965-68
108 IV	189	300SE sedan	1965-67
108 V28	130	280S	1967-72
108 E28	130	280SE/SEL sedan	1967-72
108 E35	116	280SE/SEL 3.5	1970-72
108 E45	117	280SEL 4.5	1971-72
109 III	189	300SE coupe, convertible	1966-67
109 E28	189	300SEL	1967-70
109 E35/1	116	300SEL 3.5	1969-72
109 E45	117	300SEL 4.5	1971-72
109 E63	100	300SEL 6.3	1968-71
110	121	200	1965-68
110	OM 621	220D	1965-68 (oel motor, diesel)
110	180	230	1965-68
111/1	180	220b	1959-65
111/2	180	220Sb	1959-65

Chassis	Engine	Model	Year
111/3	127	220SEb	1959-65
111 1A	180	230S	1965-68
111 III	129	250SE coupe, convertible	1965-67
111 E28	130	280SE coupe, convertible	1967-71
111 E35/1	116	280SE 3.5 sedan	1969-71
112/3	189	300SE	1961-67
113	127	230SL	1963-67
113A	129	250SL	1966-68
113 E28	130	280SL	1967-71
114 V25	114	250	1967-72
115 V22	115	220	1967-73
116 E45	117	450SE, 450SEL	1973-
116 E69	100	450SEL 6.9	1975-80
116	OM 617	300SD	1977-80
121 II	121	190SL	1955-63
123	OM 617	300D	1975-
123	OM 617A	300DT	1979-
126	OM 617A	300SD	1980-
126	116	380SEL, 380SEC	1983-
126	117	500SEL, 500SEC	1983-
128	180	220SE	1958-60
136 IV	136	170S sedan, convertible	1949-52
136 VIII	136	170SV	1953-55
180 I	180	220a	1954-56
180 II	180	220S	1956-59
186 II-III	186	300, 300b sedan	1951-55
186 IV	186	300c sedan, convertible	1955-56
187	180	220 sedan, convertible	1951-55
188 I	188	300S	1951-55
188 II	188	300Sc	1955-58
189	189	300d sedan, convertible	1957-62
198 I	198	300SL coupe	1954-57
198 II	198	300SL roadster	1957-63
201	102	190E	1983-

If you would like to attempt to master the entire model designation system, refer to W. Robert Nitske's book, *Mercedes-Benz Production Models, 1946-83.* For more comprehensive information on the earlier cars try Werner Oswald's *Mercedes-Benz Personenwagen 1886-1984.*

Parts, services and accessories

Those of you considering an older model undoubtedly are curious about the availability of parts, and rightly so. The wide variety of Mercedes-Benz models can make finding the right part difficult, but usually not impossible. Many mechanical parts are still available from Mercedes-Benz dealers; however, they are usually expensive. If you go to a dealer for a mechanical part, you will need to know the engine and chassis number. This is because many parts were modified within a model run or even a model year. Bumper and trim parts are the toughest to find—for some reason, older Mercedes-Benz bumpers seemed to be more susceptible to damage than bumpers on other cars.

It is far easier to restore an old Mercedes-Benz today than it was just a few years ago.

As the older cars become more desirable and restorations more numerous, more and more aftermarket manufacturers and suppliers have begun to supply old parts. In future years, it will likely be even easier to restore an old model.

Used parts are best found in junkyards on the East and West coasts. Complete parts cars are sometimes available from enthusiasts, usually for a reasonable price.

The following list contains sources of parts, restoration and service shops in the United States. These are not recommendations, but are just names and addresses. It is strongly suggested that you look around to find out who will give you the best quality for your dollar.

ALABAMA
Stuttgart Accessories, Inc.
600 7th St. N.
Birmingham, AL 35203
wood replacement kits

ARIZONA
Dare Carrying Case
7755 E. Redfield Rd.,
    Suite 600
Scottsdale, AZ 85260
reproduction luggage

CALIFORNIA
A-E West
P.O. Box 862
Beverly Hills, CA 90213
SL rear seats

Beverly Hills Motoring
    Accessories
200 S. Robertson Blvd.
Beverly Hills, CA 90211
general accessories

Borla
2639 Saddle Ave.
Oxnard, CA 93030
new stainless steel exhaust
    systems

Carlamb, Inc.
27 Fremont Dr.
Sonoma, CA 95476
sheepskin seat covers

Charles Brahms
P.O. Box 7395
Newport Beach, CA 92658
300 series parts

Charles Siegfried
659 Cherry St.
Santa Rosa, CA 95404
old Becker radio repair

European Parts Specialists
828 E. Ortega
Santa Barbara, CA 93103
new parts

Hill & Vaughn
1607 Lincoln Blvd.
Santa Monica, CA 90404
total restorations

JAM Engineering
P.O. Box 2570
Monterey, CA 93940
Weber carburetor kits

John Moulton
JAM Engineering
P.O. Box 2570
Monterey, CA 93940
carburetor replacement kits

Metric Automotive
18422 Oxnard St.
Tarzana, CA 91356
rebuilt engines

Miller's Mercedes Parts
17450-A Mt. Herrmann
Fountain Valley, CA 92708
new 190SL parts

Motor Sheep
5466 Complex St., #203
San Diego, CA 92123
sheepskin seat covers

Palo-Alto Speedometer
718 Emerson St.
Palo Alto, CA 94301
instruments and rebuilding

PCA Products
1726 E. Rosslynn Ave.
Fullerton, CA 92634
alloy wheels

Peter Thomas
1339 Starbush Ln.
San Jose, CA 95118
300SL used parts

Precision Auto Designs
191 Kennedy Ave.
Campbell, CA 95008-9990
hardtop hoists, trim

Robert W. Wood, Inc.
1340 Club View Dr.
Los Angeles, CA 90024
new alloy wheels

Ronal
15692 Computer Ln.
Huntington Beach, CA 92649
alloy wheels

Rudolph Axford
P.O. Box 5122
Ocean Park, CA 90405
hardtops

Scheel California Inc.
17101 S. Central Ave., Unit 1
Carson, CA 90746
seats

Scott Restorations
Scott Grundfor
14661 Lanark St.
Panoram City, CA 91402
restorations

Silver Star Executive
  Enterprises
Box 975
Highland, CA 92346
parts, service directory

Sun Valley Dismantelers
11203 Tuxford St.
Sun Valley, CA 91362
used parts, all models

XK-SS Inc.
P.O. Box 4857
Thousand Oaks, CA 91359
upholstery materials

COLORADO
Toad Hall Motorbooks
Frank Barrett
1235 Pierce St.
Lakewood, CO 80214
books

Restoration Services
27116 Mountain Park Rd.
Evergreen, CO 80439
total restorations

CONNECTICUT
Timevalve Mfg. Co.
David Opperman
P.O. Box 1615
Plainfield, CT 06374
stainless steel exhaust
  systems

FLORIDA
Autohaus Parts
913 49th St. S.
Gulfport, FL 33707
rebuilt diesel engines

Eurosport Daytona
743 S. Nova Rd.
Ormond Beach, FL 32074

Noel's
P.O. Box 7126
Orlando, FL 32854
used parts, rebuilt engines,
  transmissions

GEORGIA
AAA Inc.
2511 Forest Pkwy.
Ellenwood, GA 30049
all used parts

The Benz Store
4317 Buford Hwy.
Chamblee, GA 30341
new and used parts

ILLINOIS
AMG of North America
P.O. Box 346
Westmont, IL 60559
high-performance new parts

Delfast Corporation
1528 W. Armitrage Ave.
Chicago, IL 60622
floor mats

Paul Dauer
P.O. Box 2670
Chicago, IL 60690
old sale literature, manuals

MARYLAND
Hall Miller
19502 Burlingame Way
Gaithersburg, MD 20879
specializes in 300 used parts

MASSACHUSETTS
Alex Dearborn
Box R
Prides Crossing, MA 01965
buying, selling, appraising
  cars

Auto Enthusiasts
228 Everett Ave.
Chelsea, MA 02150
SL rear seats

Gullwing Service Co.
Paul Russell
106 Western Ave.
Essex, MA 01929
restorations

Paul's Autohaus
P.O. Box 978
Amherst, MA 01004
new mechanical and
    electrical parts

MICHIGAN
K&K Mfg. & Restorations
1560 10 Mile Rd.
Sparta, MI 49345
total restorations

Precious Metal Restorations
1732 Monroe N.W.
Grand Rapids, MI 49505
total restorations

Prestige Ltd.
23375 Dequindre
Hazel Park, MI 48030
hubcaps

MINNESOTA
Preserve Auto
6225 295 St.
Stacy, MN 55079
total restorations

MISSOURI
Passport Transport
2551 Metro Blvd.
St. Louis, MO 63043
auto transportation

Restorations Ltd.
1809 Beltway Dr.
St. Louis, MO 63114
total restorations

NEVADA
Adams Engine Service
Sparks, NV 89431
total restorations

Harrah's Automobile
    Collection
Box 10
Reno, NV 89504
total restorations

Vintage Mercedes Parts
Warren Hoar
P.O. Box 1149M
Dayton, NV 89403
prewar parts

NEW JERSEY
Bill Hirsch
396 Littleton Ave.
Newark, NJ 07103
tops and upholstery material

Hibernia Auto Restoration
Maple Terrace
Hibernia, NJ 07842
total restorations

Kanter Auto Products
76 Monroe St.
Boonton, NJ 07005
general parts and supplies

Martin Lihl
760 Ravenhill Pl.
Ridgefield, NJ 07657
wooden shift knobs

Mercedes-Benz of North
    America, Inc.
One Mercedes Dr.
Montvale, NJ 07645
technical manuals

Precision Autoworks
Bob Platz
22nd and Federal Sts.
East Camden, NJ 08105
restorations

Stan Coleman, Inc.
320 South St., Bldg. 12A
Morristown, NJ 07960
tops and upholstery material

NEW YORK
BBS of America, Inc.
33 Murray Hill Dr.
Spring Valley, NY 10977
new alloy wheels

Great Sheep Company
93 N. Park Ave.
Rockville Centre, NY 11570
sheepskin seat covers

Kozak
97 S. Lyon St.
Batavia, NY 14020
cleaning cloths

Mark Wallach Ltd.
27 New St.
Nyack, NY 10960
wood restoration

Ohara Plastics
4978 Skyline Dr.
Syracuse, NY 13215
fender liners

Stuttgart Glass
117 N. 6th St.
Lindenhurst, NY 11757
windshields

Walter Miller
315 Wedgewood Terr.
Dewitt, NY 13214
sales literature and old
    manuals

OHIO
Dayton Wheel Products
1147 S. Broadway St.
Dayton, OH 45408
wire wheels

European Motoring
    Accessories
53 E. Sycamore St.
Columbus, OH 43206
general accessories

GRM, Inc.
Jogn Grm, Jr.
1830 Henderson Dr.
Lorain, OH 44052
restorations

MIEOT/Fibertech
2995 E. 17th Ave.
Columbus, OH 43219
fiberglass body parts

PENNSYLVANIA

Comet Products
1141 Alton Pl.
Philadelphia, PA 19115
car badges

Fastcolor Images
Sandra Leitzinger
130 W. Outer Dr.
State College, PA 16801
automotive art

G&G Antique & Classic
  Autos
1440 Bristol Rd.
Hartsville, PA 18974
used 300SL parts

J. C. Taylor Antique Auto
  Insurance
320 S. 69th St.
Upper Darby, PA 19082
collector car insurance

Martin Metal Specialties
7327 State Rd.
Philadelphia, PA 19136
replating

Rick Schnitzler
Box 521
Narbeth, PA 19072
sales literature and old
  manuals

The Eastwood Company
P.O. Box 269
Malvern, PA 19355
tools and supplies

The Grundy Agency
501 Office Center Dr.
Fort Washington, PA 19034
collector car insurance

Wood Excel
532 Wellington Rd.
Norristown, PA 19403
wood restoration

RHODE ISLAND

Barry Schiff
1 Cambria Ct.
Pawtucket, RI 02860
sales literature and old
  manuals

Rhode Island Wiring Service
P.O. Box 3737
Peace Dale, RI 92883
wiring harnesses

TENNESSEE

Performance Analysis Co.
P.O. Box 109
Oak Ridge, TN 37830
oil analysis

TEXAS

German PartsHaus
1701 N. Greenville Ave.,
  #702
Richardson, TX 75081
new parts and accessories

S&S Imports
Will Sample, Jr.
3401 St. Johns Dr.
Dallas, TX 75205
new 190SL parts

VIRGINIA

Electrodyne
P.O. Box 358
Alexandria, VA 22313
general accessories

KONI America, Inc.
P.O. Box 40
Culpeper, VA 22701
shock absorbers, suspension
  kits

White Post Restorations
White Post, VA 22663
total restorations

WASHINGTON

Old Benz Barn
1424 Third W.
Seattle, WA 98119
new and used parts

WISCONSIN

A&J Auto
Monroe St.
North Hudson, WI 54016
supercharged Mercedes and
  Bugatti

Classic Motorbooks
P.O. Box 1
Osceola, WI 54020
manuals, history, reference,
  general

Clubs

USA

Mercedes-Benz Club of
America
P.O. Box 9985
Colorado Springs, CO 80932

The Mercedes-Benz Club of America is the largest Mercedes-Benz club in the world, with over 22,000 members. Its bimonthly magazine, *The Star,* is among the best of any club magazines and contains technical information, historical articles, restoration material and more. Each issue contains a four-color feature article on a selected model and carries advertisements for hundreds of Mercedes-Benz cars, accessories, parts and services. The club has 75 sections based across the United States and Canada, each one organizing its own events and meetings. Four national events are held annually, each featuring driving events and a concours d'elegance. Dues are $25 per year; ownership is not required.

Gull Wing Group
2229 Via Cerritos
Palos Verdes Estates, CA
90274

The Gull Wing Group is devoted to the preservation of 300SL roadsters and gullwing coupes. The group is also involved with reproduction of mechanical and trim parts. Main activities take place on the East and West coasts with a national convention every year. A newsletter is published monthly. Membership is approximately 900, with annual dues of $25.

West Germany

Mercedes-Benz Veteranen
Club Deutschland e.V.
Rheingaustrasse 21
6802 Landenburg, West
Germany

Mercedes-Benz Club
Oberschwaben e.V.
Schlossstrasse 33
7955 Ochsenhausen, West
Germany

Mercedes 300SL Club
Munsinger Strasse 66
7930 Ehingen 1, West
Germany

Mercedes-Benz Diesel Club
e.V.
Hauptstrasse 29
2211 Huje, West Germany

England

The Mercedes-Benz Club
Ltd.
75 Theydon Grove, Epping
Essex CM16 4PX England

France

Club Mercedes-Benz de
France
32, Rue du Docteur Mercier
F-01130 Nantau, France

Norway

Mercedes-Benz Klubben
Norge
Postboks 540
N-1301 Sanvika, Norway

Norges Mercedes-Benz Club
Torgveien 18
N-4000 Stavanger, Norway

The Netherlands

Mercedes-Benz Club
Nederland
Postbus 4275
3006 AG Rotterdam,
Holland

Austria

Mercedes SL Club Austria
Hagelingasse 13
A-1141 Vienna, Austria

Switzerland

Schweizer Mercedes-Benz
Veteranen Club Blasihof
CH-4624 Harkingen,
Switzerland

Mercedes 300SL Club
Etoile Papillon
CH-1271 Le Muids,
Switzerland

Finland
Mercedes-Benz Club
  Finnland
Puotilantie 8 F 99
SF-00910 Helsinki 91,
  Finland

Czechoslovakia
MB Club Praha (Prague)
Pisecka u. 6
Prague 3, Czechoslovakia

Brazil
Mercedes-Benz Club do
  Brasil
Rua Visconde de Praja 284,
  Apt. 504
Rio de Janeiro, Brazil

Australia
Mercedes-Benz Club ACT
P.O. Box 117
Canberra, Australia

Australian Mercedes-Benz
  Club
352 Miller Street, Sommeray
2062 Sydney, Australia

Super Star Club
P.O. Box 362, North
  Brisbane
Queensland 4000, Australia

Mercedes-Benz Car Club
P.O. Box R 122, Royal
  Exchange
New South Wales 2000,
  Australia

Japan
Mercedes-Benz Club Japan
Masao Kozu, 1581-24 Ozenji
Tama-ku, Kawasaki
Kanagawa, Japan

The Mercedes-Benz Club of
  Japan
7-6-50 Akasaka Minato-ku
Tokyo 107, Japan

Recommended reading

It is beyond the scope of this book to document each one of the vast number of Mercedes models as well as the history of DBAG. Therefore I will recommend several books and periodicals for those interested in specific models or general Mercedes-Benz history.

BOOKS

Mercedes-Benz Production Models 1946-1986 by W. Robert Nitske

A complete listing of all postwar passenger cars. Since this book was assembled by a German-American, it is especially useful in listing the models imported to the United States. The book is mainly tables and photographs, with some general historical information. Includes performance and technical specifications, original prices and production numbers.

Three-Pointed Star by David Scott-Moncrieff

The classic history of Daimler-Benz. Originally published in 1955 and extensively updated for the current third edition. Written by an Englishman, this book primarily concentrates on models available in England. Quotes, road tests, competition reports and so on are included.

Mercedes-Benz Personenwagen 1886-1984 by Werner Oswald

Although this book is presently available only in German, it is the most comprehensive list of Mercedes, Benz and Mercedes-Benz models ever compiled. If you are involved with an unusual model or just interested in the incredible range of cars built, it is a must. Includes yearly production figures and photographs of most models and body styles.

Road & Track on Mercedes Sports & GT Cars 1970-1980.
Reprinted articles.

Mercedes-Benz: A Century of Invention and Innovation by the editors of Automobile Quarterly.

Mercedes-Benz 1886-1986 by Jurgen Lewandowski.

The Star and the Laurel: The Centennial History of Daimler, Mercedes and Benz 1886-1986 by Beverly Rae Kimes.

Mercedes-Benz: The Supercharged 8-Cylinder Cars of the 1930's by Jan Melin.

Mercedes-Benz Automobile: 28/95PS to SSKL by Halwart Schrader.

Mercedes-Benz Automobile: 170V to 300SL by Halwart Schrader.

Mercedes-Benz Automobile: 190SL to 300SEL by Heribert Hofner.

Mercedes-Benz Automobile: 600 to 450SEL by Heribert Hofner.

Mercedes-Benz AutoHistory series

300SL by William Boddy
V8s by F. Wilson McComb
Roadsters by John Bolster

The Mercedes-Benz: Collector's Guides

by James Taylor
Since 1945, Volume 1
Since 1945, Volume 2: The 1960's
Since 1945, Volume 3: The 1970's

Mercedes-Benz Cars

Brooklands Books series of reprinted articles
230/250/280SL 1963-1971
350/450SL & SLC 1971-80
1949-1954
Competition Cars 1950-1957
1954-1957
1957-1961

PERIODICALS

If you are looking for, restoring or trying to sell a Mercedes-Benz, you may find these magazines useful. Most of them carry classified advertisements (cars for sale and so on) and display advertisements (parts, supplies, restoration services).

Hemmings Motor News
Monthly magazine, consists almost entirely of ads for older cars and related parts, services and so on.

In Aller Welt
Magazine of Daimler-Benz AG, bi-monthly, geared to new cars, but occasional historical pieces, no advertisements.

The Star
Mercedes-Benz Club of America, P.O. Box 9985, Colorado Springs, Colorado 80932.